Reading **Better,**
Reading **Smarter**

DEBORAH APPLEMAN AND MICHAEL F. GRAVES

Reading Better, Reading Smarter

Designing Literature Lessons for Adolescents

HEINEMANN
Portsmouth, NH

Heinemann
361 Hanover Street
Portsmouth, NH 03801–3912
www.heinemann.com

Offices and agents throughout the world

The authors and publisher wish to thank those who have generously given permission to reprint borrowed material:

Figure 1.3 "SRE for *Significant Moments in the Life of My Mother*" is reprinted by permission of Seward, Inc., Minneapolis, MN. This is a summary of an SRE developed by Seward, Inc. with funds from the U.S. Department of Education. The complete SRE and a number of other SREs are available at online-readingresources.com.

Figure 1.5 is adapted from the "Model of Explicit Instruction" in "The Instruction of Reading Comprehension" by P. D. Pearson and M. C. Gallagher, originally appearing in *Contemporary Educational Psychology*, July 1, 1983, Volume 8, Issue 3. Published by Academic Press. Reprinted by permission of Copyright Clearance Center.

Credits continue on p. x

Library of Congress Cataloging-in-Publication Data
Appleman, Deborah.
    Reading better, reading smarter : designing literature lessons for adolescents
/ Deborah Appleman and Michael F. Graves.
        p. cm.
    Includes bibliographical references.
    ISBN-13: 978-0-325-04240-4
    ISBN-10: 0-325-04240-3
    1. Reading (Secondary). 2. Literature—Study and teaching (Secondary).
3. Teenagers—Books and reading. 4. Lesson planning. I. Graves, Michael F.
II. Title.

LB1632.A674 2011
428.4071'2—dc23   2011025126

Editor: Anita Gildea
Production: Lynne Costa
Cover and interior designs: Monica Ann Crigler
Typesetter: Valerie Levy, Drawing Board Studios
Manufacturing: Steve Bernier

Printed in the United States of America on acid-free paper
15   14   13   12   11   VP   1   2   3   4   5

For John and for Bonnie.

We don't deserve your patience, but we're glad we have it.

CONTENTS

CHAPTER 2

During-Reading Activities　43

CHAPTER 3

Postreading Activities　56

CHAPTER 4

Lenses for Approaching Literary Texts　75

CHAPTER 5

Comprehensive SREs for English Classes　87

PREFACE

English Teacher and Reading Teacher

Ms. Kerr's fourth-hour tenth-grade English class is on fire. Hers is a typical urban classroom, large and strikingly diverse in every way, including reading ability. The students have just read Abraham Rodriguez, Jr.'s "The Boy Without a Flag," a contemporary story about a young Puerto Rican boy who disobeys school authorities by refusing to salute the flag. Nearly every hand is raised, as students clamor to join the discussion about whether the protagonist of the story has made the right decision. Ms. Kerr has her students stand and demonstrate their position by forming a "human barometer." Students are able to participate because they have read, comprehended, and interpreted the story. Although the story is challenging, no student seems left behind during this two-day lesson. Ms. Kerr has provided a Scaffolded Reading Experience (SRE) (Graves and Graves 2003; Graves and Fitzgerald 2009), a framework that allows her to plan a lesson specifically designed for this particular group of readers, this story, and what she wants students to gain from reading it.

Teaching Literature or Teaching Reading?

If you call yourself an English teacher and you've purchased this book, you have already conquered the first hurdle in helping all your students read successfully. You are seeking strategies beyond those of literary interpretation to help all your students make meaning of texts. You are looking for specific instructional methods to help your students become better readers. This book discusses precisely those strategies.

Historically, the language arts field has been divided between those who consider ourselves teachers of literature and those who consider ourselves teachers of reading. In fact, one of the authors of this book (Deborah) is primarily a researcher in how literature gets taught; the other (Michael) deals primarily with reading instruction. Our preservice training, our first few years of teaching, and perhaps even our natural predispositions toward reading and literature contribute to this divide. Yet the time has come to merge these two perspectives so that we may better serve *all* our students and their literacy needs.

From English Teacher to Literacy Teacher

This merging has already begun. Over the last decade or so, these two previously distinct perspectives—teaching reading and teaching literature— have begun to inform each other, both in the classroom and in literacy research. Today's literacy scholars draw on the theoretical underpinnings of both reading research and research focusing on response to literature to help teachers choose texts, establish learning environments, create lessons, and design methods of assessment that help ensure every student's reading success (Alvermann 1999; Applebee 1993; Appleman 2009, 2010; Beach and Myers 2001; Graves and Graves 2003; Kamil, Pearson, Moje, and Afflerbach 2011; Langer 1995; Lapp and Fisher 2011; Philippot and Graves 2009; Wilhelm 1997). In addition, literacy researchers have examined various factors that influence and shape students' literacy learning—from the cognitive processes involved in reading to the particular contextual factors that influence a student's reading to larger social cultural considerations that affect literacy learning. For example, recent research has explored the relationship of out-of-school contexts and literacies to school-based academic performance in reading and writing (Fisher 2007; Hull and Schultz 2001; Morrell 2004; Vasudevan and Wissman 2011) and focused on the degree to which gender influences students' reading ability and interests (Newkirk 2002; Pirie 2002; Smith and Wilhelm 2002).

Being a literature teacher now means being well versed in our growing understanding of what it means to help all students learn to read and understand all kinds of texts—from short stories, novels, and poems to newspapers and magazine articles to web pages and text messages. Being an English teacher means—and at some pragmatic level probably has always meant—helping students make meaning as they read, a goal shared by literature teachers and reading teachers.

Today's Language Arts Classroom

Today's classrooms reflect many of the demographic changes in our country. Most English classrooms are larger and more diverse than they have ever been. There are many more newcomers than there were even ten years ago. As funding for public schools has shrunk, classrooms are increasingly under-resourced, and money for new materials has become increasingly difficult to come by. More schools have larger populations of high-poverty students. Our classrooms are filled with students whose cultural backgrounds and stances toward mainstream learning practices vary widely (Bean and Harper 2011; Mahiri 2002; Ogbu 2003; Tatum 2005). Our increased ability to assess and monitor students' progress in reading, and the increased mandated reliance on standardized assessments, has helped us realize what has probably been true for decades—that our English classrooms are filled with students who read considerably below grade level, and that while students may be able to decode the texts we assign, many students may not derive as much meaning or pleasure from texts as they could simply because they are not adequately and specifically prepared to read them.

The Literacy Crisis

All of these factors have helped fuel public concern about a literacy crisis. Almost annually, federal reports such as *Adolescent Literacy Fact Sheet* (Alliance for Excellent Education 2010), *The Nation's Report Card: Reading* (National Council on Education 2009), *To Read or Not to Read: A Question of National Consequence* (National Endowment for the Arts 2008), and NCTE'S *Adolescent Literacy* research brief (2008) document the changing demands of literacy in a digital age and our collective fear that our schools are not meeting the basic literacy needs of our adolescents. Even students proficient in digital forms of literacy sometimes have difficulty transferring that proficiency to traditional literacy acts such as reading literary texts or writing essays (Beers 2003; Gee 2003). Additionally, more pressure has been placed on all classroom teachers because of mandated reporting of academic progress in reading (as well as other subjects) by the federal program No Child Left Behind. This mandated reporting is likely to be demanded in the future by new federal programs, state requirements, and the recent Common Core State Standards Initiative, which seems likely to result in more students being faced more often with very challenging texts.

Given all these factors, today's English teachers are likely to feel tugged in seemingly opposite directions. We feel a sense of urgency to do everything in our power to foster literacy practices among our students, to make certain they are successful readers and writers. Yet we worry that we will lose the texture, richness, and autonomy of our literature classrooms if our pedagogy is held hostage to standardized tests. We often still labor under the mistaken notion that kids' reading improves only through very explicit reading instruction and centralized and standardized reading programs.

Given all these factors, today's English teachers are likely to feel tugged in seemingly opposite directions. We feel a sense of urgency to do everything in our power to foster literacy practices among our students, to make certain they are successful readers and writers. Yet we worry that we will lose the texture, richness, and autonomy of our literature classrooms if our pedagogy is held hostage to standardized tests.

While there is clearly some justification for a sense of urgency with regard to adolescent literacy, English teachers do not need to succumb to a mistaken conclusion that increased attention to improving students' reading proficiency will shift the instructional focus from literature to "drill and skill." Moreover, while the Common Core Standards for sixth- through eleventh-grade students state that "students will be able to read and comprehend literature, including stories, dramas, and poems . . . with scaffolding as needed at the high end of the [text complexity] range," they do not discuss what effective scaffolding might look like. The framework offered in this book—the Scaffolded Reading Experience—should therefore be particularly appealing to teachers of literature. Scaffolded Reading Experiences (SREs) are not a comprehensive reading instruction program. Instead, SREs are an important part of a balanced, intentional approach to reading and literature instruction. Rather than replacing the literature content of an English curriculum, SREs enrich, highlight, and revitalize that curriculum. Moreover, SREs can be used to differentiate instruction for the full range of students in today's English classes.

Scaffolded Reading Experiences

Scaffolded Reading Experiences are based on several decades of research on the importance of instructional scaffolding and the application of that concept to reading texts. Educational researchers have refined the notion of scaffolding, first associated with the development of verbal abilities in very young children, so that it now applies to students of all ages and all abilities. A scaffold is a "temporary and adjustable support that enables the accomplishment of a task that would be impossible without the scaffold's support" (Anderson 1989). The SRE framework is solidly grounded on this bedrock concept. SREs help place readers in what Vygotsky (1978) called the *zone of proximal development*. That is, SREs provide the conceptual and cognitive support that helps students read and interpret texts that are within their developmental reach but would be difficult if attempted without support.

SREs help students read texts successfully, enjoyably, and purposefully. Each SRE is designed for a particular text, a particular instructional context, and a particular purpose or set of purposes. The primary components are prereading, during-reading, and postreading activities. These emphases are familiar to all teachers of literature. Before we read a literary text with our students, we often motivate them, preview the selection, and activate their relevant prior knowledge. While our students are reading a text, we often guide their reading, point out relevant textual features, and encourage them to internalize the heuristic practices that good readers automatically practice (Schoenbach, Greenleaf, Cziko, and Hurwitz 1999). After reading, we provide opportunities for students to reflect on the meaning they have made and to connect this particular reading experience to other reading they have done as well as to life experiences. Teachers of literature have long considered these three phases of pre-, during- and postreading in their instruction (Beach and Myers 2001).

SREs Can Transform How You Teach Literature

What do SREs offer that's new? In typical pre-, during-, and postreading instruction, the same set of activities are used over and over, without regard for the students, the text, and the purpose for which students are reading. SREs, on the other hand, are specifically tailored to our instruction. There are many kinds of pre-, while-, and postreading activities, and we can combine and design each component based on:

- **the abilities and characteristics of each particular group of readers,**
- **the characteristics, content, and difficulty of each literary text, and**
- **what we expect students to gain from the reading experience.**

Students' reading success depends on many factors, but text selection is of primary importance. SREs inform text selection in several ways:

1. They help us assess the suitability of specific literary texts for your particular students.

2. They offer powerful new ways of making familiar but sometimes difficult and inaccessible literary chestnuts come alive.

3. They show you how you might adapt the teaching of a particular text to different learning contexts.

Using SREs can help you become more intentional about what we are doing to help our students become better readers. After all, we are teaching *students*, not texts.

Overview of This Book

The introduction defines a Scaffolded Reading Experience and briefly explains its components.

Chapter 1, "Prereading Activities"; Chapter 2, " During-Reading Activities"; and Chapter 3, "Postreading Activities," present numerous examples of specific pre-, while-, and postreading activities appropriate for English classes.

Chapter 4, "Lenses for Approaching Literary Texts," takes up theoretical concerns specific to teaching literature, including how to incorporate the explicit teaching of contemporary literary theory into the design and implementation of SREs.

Chapter 5, "Comprehensive SREs for English Classes," presents complete sets of pre-, during-, and postreading activities for four familiar and widely used texts: a short story, a novel, a poem, and an expository piece.

Finally, Chapter 6, "Selecting Texts and Assessing Student Performance," helps you evaluate and assess the difficulty of texts you are currently teaching and/or may consider teaching in the future. It also describes formal and informal ways of evaluating student performance.

A Final Word

The specific and detailed descriptions and examples of SREs in the later chapters are neither blueprints nor prescriptions to be followed exactly. They animate the principles behind SREs and are models you can use to develop similar activities. They are a modest starting point for the imaginative and creative lessons you will design as you apply this flexible framework to some of your favorite texts as well as new ones. As Ms. Kerr and her students have discovered, there is an important place for SREs in English classrooms in which students learn to love and appreciate literature as they become better and smarter readers.

INTRODUCTION

What Is a Scaffolded Reading Experience?

Mr. Slater looked out at his new class of sixth graders and allowed himself a little sigh, whether of contentment or concern he wasn't sure. His students were fully engaged in an activity he uses at the beginning of the year to get some insight into their writing proficiency, and this was a positive sign. On the other hand, he knew from their records and from the group discussions the class had had thus far that this was going to be a challenging year for many of these students and for him. Mr. Slater was new to the school, having recently moved to the area. The curriculum his sixth-grade colleagues had agreed on was challenging: novels, for example, included Christopher Paul Curtis' *The Watsons Go to Birmingham—1963*, Lauren Myracle's *ttyl*, and Adam Rapp's *Under the Wolf, Under the Dog*. He had taught *The Watsons* before, but never *ttyl* or *Under the Wolf, Under the Dog*, and when he read them just before school began he knew they would require a lot of work, both by him and by his students. Still, armed with the Scaffolded Reading Experience framework, he was confident his students would be able to read these books successfully. He sighed again. This time it was definitely one of contentment. Helping students meet challenging reading tasks was his thing.

What Is a Scaffolded Reading Experience?

An SRE is a flexible plan that you tailor to a specific situation— to your students, the texts you use, and what you want students to glean from their reading

A Scaffolded Reading Experience is a set of prereading, during-reading, and postreading activities individually created to assist a particular group of students in successfully reading, understanding, learning from, and enjoying a particular selection. Tierney and Readence (2005) classify the Scaffolded Reading Experience and other such plans as "lesson frameworks," and this is an appropriate classification. But an SRE differs markedly from most other instructional frameworks in that it is not a preset or largely preset plan for dealing with a text. Instead, an SRE is a flexible plan that you tailor to a specific situation—to your students, the texts you use, and what you want students to glean from their reading.

It has two parts, as shown in the following figure. The first part, the planning phase, takes into consideration the particular group of students doing the reading, the text they are reading, and their purpose or purposes for reading it. The second part, the implementation phase, provides a set of prereading, during-reading, and postreading options for those particular readers, the selection being read, and the purposes of the reading. Different situations call for different SREs.

Two Phases of a Scaffolded Reading Experience

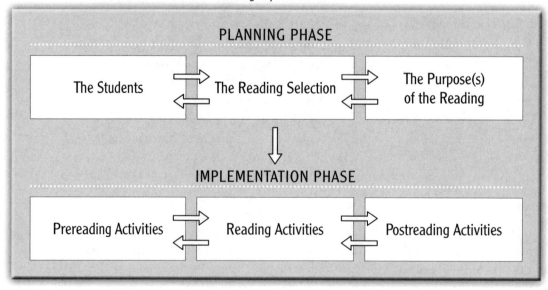

As shown, the first phase of the SRE is the planning phase, during which you plan and create the entire experience. The second phase is the implementation phase, the activities you and your students engage in as a result of your planning. This two-phase process is a vital feature of the SRE approach in that the planning phase allows you to tailor each SRE you create to the specific situation you face. Different situations call for different SREs.

Suppose you are working with a typical class of seniors, and you want them to develop some thorough understanding and real appreciation for Yann Martel's *The Life of Pi*. Or consider a very different situation. Suppose you are working with these same seniors and your purpose is to have them decide whether they would like to read a memoir of growing up in the 1950s, Bill Bryson's *The Life and Times of the Thunderbolt Kid*, as a class text.

In each of these situations, your planning leads to the creation of the SRE itself and to your implementing it, but the two SREs will differ markedly. As shown in the lower half of the figure on page 4, the components of the implementation phase are prereading, during-reading, and postreading activities. With *The Life of Pi*, we have already suggested that you want students to develop a thorough understanding and appreciation. This means that your SRE for *The Life of Pi* is likely to be a substantial one, with prereading activities that prepare students to understand and appreciate this challenging text, during-reading activities that lead them to interact with the text in ways that help them respond to Pi's bizarre adventure and view of the world, and postreading activities that give them opportunities to check their understanding of the text and consider the author's craft. To accomplish all this, the class might spend several weeks reading the novel and completing the learning activities you have assembled.

On the other hand, with the first chapter of Bryson's memoir and the major goal of students simply deciding whether they would like to read the whole of the book, your SRE is likely to be minimal. Prereading might consist of an introduction to the '50s, to Bryson, and to memoir as a genre; students might read the chapter silently to themselves; and postreading might consist of discussion of whether this or other memoirs might be a good read for the class. In this case, the class might spend only a period reading and discussing the chapter.

In addition to recognizing that the SRE framework results in very different SREs for different situations, it is important to recognize that the components of each phase of the SRE are interrelated. Consider the three components of the planning phase—the students, the text, and your purposes. If you are faced with a specific text and purposes for reading it, as you may be if your school adheres to a Common Core Standards framework, then you need to make that text accessible to all of your students, as well as create ways that all of them can

It is important to recognize that the components of each phase of the SRE are interrelated.

Possible Components of a Scaffolded Reading Experience

PREREADING ACTIVITIES

1. Motivating
2. Relating the Reading to Students' Lives
3. Activating and Building Background Knowledge
4. Providing Text-Specific Knowledge
5. Preteaching Vocabulary
6. Preteaching Concepts
7. Prequestioning, Predicting, and Setting Direction
8. Suggesting Strategies
9. Considering Literary Elements
10. Suggesting Literary Lenses

DURING-READING ACTIVITIES

11. Silent Reading
12. Reading to Students
13. Supported Reading
14. Traditional Study Activities
15. Student Oral Reading
16. Modifying the Text

POSTREADING ACTIVITIES

17. Questioning
18. Discussion
19. Writing
20. Drama
21. Artistic, Graphic, and Nonverbal Activities
22. Application and Outreach Activities
23. Building Connections
24. Reteaching

achieve those purposes. The same sort of interdependency holds with the three components of the implementation phase. For example, if you decide you are going to have some very challenging postreading tasks, you'll want to include prereading activities and during-reading activities that thoroughly prepare students to accomplish those challenging tasks.

The possible pre-, during-, and postreading components of an SRE are listed in the figure on p. 4. Before continuing, we want to stress two facts about this list. First, although many of the components we list can occur at various points in an SRE (pre, during, and/or post), each is listed only once, either at the position in which it is most likely to occur or in the position at which it is likely to first occur. Second, these are *possible* components of an SRE. No single SRE would include anything like all of these activities.

Prereading Activities

Prereading activities prepare students to read a selection. They can serve a number of functions, including:

- **getting students interested in reading the selection,**
- **reminding students of things they already know that will help them understand and enjoy the selection, and**
- **preteaching aspects of the selection that may be difficult.**

Prereading activities are particularly important because with adequate preparation the experience of reading will be enjoyable, rewarding, and successful. Prereading activities are widely recommended (Alvermann, Phelps, and Gillis 2010; Beach and Myers 2001; Beers 2003; Echevarria, Vogt, and Short 2007; Englert et al. 2007; Goldenberg and Coleman 2010; Graves, Juel, Graves, and Dewitz 2011; Jago 2004; Langer 1995; Olson 2010; Readence, Moore, and Rickelman 2000; Schoenbach, Greenleaf, Cziko, and Huriwtz 1999; Smith and Wilhelm 2002; Snow 2001; Wilhelm, Baker, and Dube 2002; Wilhelm 1997), and a number of different types of prereading activities have been suggested. In creating the list of possible prereading activities for SREs, we have attempted to list a relatively small set of categories that suggest a large number of useful activities teachers and students can engage in. As shown in the list of SRE components, we suggest ten types.

1. *Motivating* activities include anything designed to interest students. Although a variety of prereading activities can be motivational as well as accomplish some other purpose, we list motivating activities as a separate category because we believe that it is perfectly appropriate to do something solely for the purpose of motivating students. In fact, we believe that motivating activities should be used frequently.

2. ***Relating the reading to students' lives*** is so self-evident an activity that we don't need to say much about it. We will, though, point out that, because showing students how a selection relates to them is such a powerful motivator and promotes comprehension, it is something we like to do often.

3. ***Activating or building background knowledge*** ensures that students get the most from what they read. When you activate background knowledge, you prompt students to consciously recall information they already know that will help them understand the text. For example, let's say a group of eighth graders is researching the plight of migrant workers. Before they read a story from *The Circuit,* Francisco Jiménez's award-winning collection of stories based on his own experiences as a child migrant worker in California, you might encourage them to discuss what they have already learned about migrant workers from their previous reading.

    In addition to activating background knowledge, it is sometimes necessary to *build* background knowledge, knowledge the author assumes readers already possess. For example, in his stories Jiménez presupposes some specific knowledge of California geography. If you think your eighth graders don't know this information, supplying it makes good sense.

4. ***Providing text-specific knowledge*** differs from activating or building background knowledge in that it gives students information that is contained in the reading selection itself. Providing students with advance information on the content of a selection—giving students the seven topics discussed in an article on characterization, for example—may be justified if the selection is difficult or densely packed with information. This of course is likely to be increasingly the case as schools respond to the Common Core State Standards Initiative.

5. ***Preteaching vocabulary*** refers to preteaching new labels for concepts that students already know. For example, you are teaching vocabulary—introducing a new label—if you teach your tenth graders that the word *jettison* means "to throw something from a ship, aircraft, or other vehicle." It often makes sense to take a few minutes and preteach a half-dozen new vocabulary words before students read a selection.

6. ***Preteaching concepts*** is a different matter (Graves 2009). Preteaching concepts refers to preteaching new and potentially challenging ideas, not just new labels for ideas students already understand. For example, the full meaning of *tragedy* is a new concept for eighth graders. Teaching new and difficult concepts takes significant amounts of time and requires powerful instruction. It does not make sense to attempt to preteach a half-dozen new and difficult concepts in a few minutes.

7. ***Prequestioning, predicting, and setting direction*** are similar activities. With any of them, you are focusing students' attention and telling them what is important to look for as they read.

8. ***Suggesting strategies*** is another appropriate prereading activity. The key word here is *suggesting*. SREs are not designed to *teach* strategies—instructing students how to do something they could not previously do almost always requires more time than we allot to SREs. However, it is often appropriate to suggest as part of an SRE that students use strategies they already know. For example, you might suggest to seventh graders reading a selection that presents a complex argument that it would be a good idea to summarize the argument in their own words.

9. ***Considering literary elements*** is one more possible component of an SRE. This time, the key word is *considering*. SREs are not designed to initially *teach* literary elements. We are assuming that the concepts and procedures involved in recognizing and making use of literary elements have been taught at some previous time. In an SRE you are asking students to work with some ideas they are already familiar with as they read a particular text. Consciously considering the literary elements of a text—genre, setting, characterization, plot structure, point of view, and so on—helps students both comprehend and interpret it. For instance, understanding basic plot structure helps students recognize, anticipate, and predict narrative developments as they read a story. We suggest that, rather than invoking all literary elements with each work, you focus on no more than two or three with each text.

10. ***Suggesting literary lenses*** is the final prereading activity we suggest here. As with the previous two activities, this one assumes that you are dealing with concepts already taught. Literary lenses are perspectives that show students how different readers might interpret the same text differently. Literary perspectives help us understand what is important to individual readers, and they show us why those readers end up seeing what they see. Students can think of literary perspectives as lenses through which they can examine a text. Frequently used literary perspectives that you might easily incorporate into an SRE include gender, social power, reader response, biographical, historical, and archetypal.

Note that although we list each type of activity only once, activities often span several parts of an SRE.

In concluding this section on prereading activities, we would like to again note that although we list each type of activity only once, activities often span several parts of an SRE. For example, while we are likely to ask students to consider certain literary elements before they read a selection, they are going to be considering the elements as they are actually reading, and probably discussing them after they read.

During-Reading Activities

During-reading activities include both things that students themselves do as they are reading and things that you do to assist them as they are reading. Like prereading activities, during-reading activities are frequently recommended (Beach and Myers 2001; Bean, Valerio, and Stevens 1999; Beers 2003; Echevarria, Vogt, and Short 2007; Englert et al. 2007; Goldenberg and Coleman 2010; Graves, Juel, Graves, and Dewitz 2011; Jago 2004; Langer 1995; Olson 2010; Readence, Moore, and Rickelman 2000; Richardson 2000; Roser, Martinez, and Wood 2011; Schoenbach, Greenleaf, Cziko, and Huriwtz 1999; Smith and Wilhelm 2002; Snow 2001; Wilhelm, Baker, and Dube 2002; Wilhelm 2008; Wood, Lapp, and Flood 1992). In creating the list of possible during-reading activities for SREs, we have again attempted to list relatively few types that suggest a large number of useful activities. As shown in the list of possible SRE components on p. 4, we suggest six types.

1. *Silent reading* is listed first because it both *is* and *should be* the most frequently used during-reading activity. The central long-term goal of literature instruction is to prepare students to become accomplished lifelong readers, and the vast majority of the reading adults do is silent. It is both a basic rule of learning and common sense that one needs to repeatedly practice the skill he or she is attempting to master. If you choose appropriate selections for students to read and have adequately prepared them to read the selections, students will often be able to read the selections silently on their own.

2. *Reading to students* serves a number of functions, even in the middle and secondary grades. Hearing a story or other text read aloud is a very pleasurable experience and is also a model of good oral reading. Reading the first chapter or the first few pages of a piece can ease students into the material and entice them to read the rest of the selection on their own. Reading aloud to students who find certain texts difficult—or having them listen to an audiotape, CD, or MP3 file—can make the material more accessible. Many less-proficient readers and some (but by no means all) English learners find listening easier than reading.

3. *Supported reading* focuses students' attention on particular aspects of a text as they read it. Supported reading often begins as a prereading activity—perhaps with you setting a direction—and is then carried out while students read. For example, if you find that an expository piece on characterization is actually divided into half a dozen sections but contains no headings or subheadings, you might give students a semantic map that includes titles for the half dozen sections and ask them to complete the map as they are reading. Often, with supported reading activities, students'

goal is to learn something from their reading rather than just read for enjoyment. Thus, supported reading activities are frequently used with expository material. However, it is also possible to guide students in understanding and responding to narratives, for example, to help sixth graders recognize the plot structure of the Newbery award–winning novel, *A Single Shard*, by Linda Sue Park, or to help twelfth graders understand and appreciate the surreal imagery, flashbacks, dream sequences, and extended poetic passages in Sherman Alexie's interconnected set of thought-provoking stories *The Lone Ranger and Tonto Fist Fight in Heaven*.

4. *Traditional study activities* include things like taking notes, underlining, and jotting notes in the margin, which have served many students well over the years and still have a place in the classroom. They differ from supported reading in that students generally work independently.

5. *Student oral reading* isn't done very often in most English classrooms, because the vast majority of reading that secondary students do in school and will do as adults is silent. Nonetheless, oral reading has its place. Poetry is often best appreciated and most effective when read orally. Also, poignant or particularly well-written passages of prose are often best savored when read aloud. Reading orally can help a class or group of students decide between alternate interpretations of a passage or recognize what is and is not explicitly stated. Additionally, students often like to read their own writing orally. And, of course, having individual students read orally provides valuable insights about their reading competence.

6. *Modifying the text* is sometimes necessary to make lengthy or difficult material more accessible. Modifying the text might mean presenting the material on audio- or videotapes, changing the format, simplifying it, or having students read only certain parts. Assuming students can and will read the original, will they get as much out of reading a modified version or listening to it on tape? Almost certainly not! But if they cannot or will not read the original in its entirety, hearing it read or reading part of it successfully is preferable to not reading it at all.

Postreading Activities

Postreading activities serve a variety of purposes:

- **They provide opportunities for students to synthesize and organize information gleaned from the text so that they can understand and recall important points.**

- **They provide opportunities for students to evaluate an author's message, his or her stance in presenting a message, and the quality of the text itself.**

- **They provide opportunities for you and your students to evaluate their understanding of the text.**
- **They provide opportunities for students to respond to a text in a variety of ways—to reflect on the meaning of the text, to compare differing texts and ideas, to imagine themselves as one of the characters in the text, to synthesize information from different sources, to engage in a variety of creative activities, and to apply what they have learned within the classroom walls to the world beyond the classroom.**

Students need to be able to read something without facing some sort of accountability afterward.

Not surprisingly, given their many functions, postreading activities are also widely recommended (Alvermann 2000; Beach and Myers 2001; Bean, Valerio, and Stevens 1999; Beers 2003; Echevarria, Vogt, and Short 2007; Englert et al. 2007; Gambrell and Almasi 1996; Goldenberg and Coleman 2010; Graves, Juel, Graves, and Dewitz 2011; Jago 2004; Langer 1995; Olson 2010; Readence, Moore, and Rickelman 2000; Schoenbach, Greenleaf, Cziko, and Huriwtz 1999; Smith and Wilhelm 2002; Snow 2001; Wilhelm, Baker, and Dube 2002; Wilhelm 2008; Wood, Lapp, and Flood 1992), and in most classrooms they are very frequently used. In creating the list of possible postreading activities for SREs, we have once again attempted to list a relatively small number of types— eight in this case—that suggest a large number of useful activities:

1. *Questioning*, either orally or in writing, is frequently warranted. Posing questions encourages and promotes higher-order thinking—it nudges students to interpret, analyze, and evaluate what they have read. Questions can also elicit creative and personal responses: *How did you feel when . . . ? What do you think the main character would have done if . . . ?* Sometimes, of course, students need to be able to read something without facing some sort of accountability afterward. However, many times neither you nor your students will be sure they have gained what they needed to gain from the reading without their answering some questions. Of course, teachers shouldn't be the only ones asking the questions. Students can ask questions of each other, they can ask us questions, and they can ask themselves questions they plan to answer through further reading or by searching the Internet.

2. *Discussion*, whether in pairs, in small groups, or as a class, is a very frequent and often very appropriate activity. If there is a chance that some students did not understand as much of what they read as they need to—and this is often the case—discussion is definitely warranted. Equally important, discussion is a chance for students to offer their personal interpretations and responses and hear those of others. Discussion is also useful for assessing whether reading goals have been achieved and evaluate

what went right with the reading experience, what went wrong, and what might be done differently in the future.

3. *Writing* probably ought to be used more frequently than it is. Over the past thirty years, there has been a good deal of well-warranted emphasis on reading and writing as complementary activities that should often be dealt with together. We certainly agree. However, writing is often challenging, and it is important to be sure that students are adequately prepared. Among other things, this means that if students are expected to write about a selection, you usually need to be sure they have understood it well. We say *usually* because sometimes students can write to discover or deepen what they have understood.

4. *Drama*—any sort of performance involving action and movement— includes a range of opportunities that allow students to respond actively to what they have read. Short plays, skits, pantomimes, and readers' theatre are some of the many possibilities.

5. *Artistic, graphic, and nonverbal activities* include visual arts, graphic arts, music, dance, and media productions such as videos, slide shows, and audiotapes, as well as construction activities not typically thought of as artistic. They most frequently involve creating graphics of some sort— maps, charts, diagrams, PowerPoint presentations, and the like. Other possibilities include constructing models or bringing in artifacts relevant to the selection read. Artistic and nonverbal activities are fun to do, are breaks from typical school tasks, and allow students of varying talents and abilities to express themselves in ways in which they excel.

6. *Application and outreach activities* include both direct, concrete applications—cooking something after reading a recipe—and less direct, less concrete ones—attempting to change some aspect of student government after reading about something in state or national government that suggests the possibility. Here, we include off-campus activities— conducting a drive to collect used coats and sweaters after reading a news article on people in need of winter clothing, or taking a field trip to a local art museum after reading about one of the artists exhibited there. Obviously, there is a great range of options.

7. *Building connections* overlaps somewhat with application and outreach activities. Nevertheless, we list it as its own category because building connections is so important. Only by helping students build connections between the ideas they encounter in literature and other parts of their lives can we ensure that they come to really value literature, see the relevance of literature, remember and apply important things they've learned from the literature they read, and make literature a vital part of their adult lives. Several sorts of connections are important:

◆ First, we want students to connect the wealth of out-of-school experiences they bring to school with their reading—for example, to relate the pride they felt in learning to drive a stick shift with the pride a story character feels when she meets a difficult challenge.

◆ Second, we want students to connect what they learn in one subject with what they learn in others. For example, they might use the narrator's dilemma in deciding whether to report for induction or flee to Canada during the Vietnam War in Tim O'Brien's "On the Rainy River" to better understand resistance to the Vietnam War as discussed in their history text.

◆ Third, we want them to realize that concepts they learn from literature can apply well beyond the classroom—for example, that just as a fictional character's perseverance brought her success, so their perseverance at the real-life tasks they face can bring them success.

8. ***Reteaching*** is the final postreading activity we discuss. When it becomes apparent that students have not achieved their reading goals or the level of understanding you deem necessary, reteaching is often in order, and the best time is usually as soon as possible after students first encounter the material. In some cases, reteaching may consist simply of asking students to reread parts of a selection. In other cases, you may want to present a minilesson on a problematic part of the text. And in still other cases, students who have understood a particular aspect of the text may help other students reach a similar understanding.

Variability in Scaffolded Reading Experiences

We've already noted that our list of pre-, during-, and postreading activities is a set of options, that no single SRE will include all these options, and that SREs will vary considerably. Here's a concrete example.

Consider first a very sturdy SRE for a challenging text. Suppose you are working with a class of talented seniors. The class is reading Margaret Atwood's "Significant Moments in the Life of My Mother." The SRE in the next figure was designed by Martha Cosgrove, a teacher at Edina High School, in Minnesota. Clearly, this brief outline reveals only the broad form of the SRE, but five characteristics are clear:

1. It spans five days.
2. It includes fifteen separate activities.
3. The activities have been selected based on Martha's assessment of a particular group of students.
4. The activities have been chosen based on the story the students are reading.
5. This combination of prereading, during-reading, and postreading activities is only one of a number of combinations Martha could have selected.

Martha Cosgrove's SRE Supporting Margaret Atwood's "Significant Moments in the Life of My Mother"

DAY 1

PREREADING ACTIVITIES

1. *Relating the reading to students' lives:* Think about the people who have most influenced you. List them rapidly in no particular order. *(10 minutes)*
2. *Impromptu writing practice:* Pick one of the people who you listed above and write about his or her sphere of influence on you. *(25 minutes)*
3. *Building background knowledge:* Focus on the words *significant* and *moments* and consider why Atwood might have chosen those words for her title. *(15 minutes)*

DURING-READING ACTIVITY (HOMEWORK)

4. Read the story and the record the events that occur.

(continues)

(continued)

DAY 2

POSTREADING ACTIVITIES

5. *Discussion in pairs:* What is revealed about the characters thus far? *(15 minutes)*
6. *Whole-class discussion:* What did you learn about the characters from the paired discussion? What "things" linked to gender are used to identify them? *(35 minutes)*
7. *Homework:* Record "men things" and "women things" brought up in the discussion.

DAY 3

POSTREADING ACTIVITIES (CONT'D)

8. *Check homework. (10 minutes)*
9. *Whole-class discussion:* How do we come to assign gender to particular objects? *(30 minutes)*
10. *Investigate author background:* In what ways is Margaret Atwood a feminist writer? *(15 minutes)*

DAY 4

POSTREADING ACTIVITIES (CONT'D)

11. *Discussion of literary techniques:* Discuss characterization and theme, focusing specifically on how to distinguish statements of theme from statements of subject. *(30 minutes)*
12. *Prewriting activity:* Brainstorm three or four incidents that involve a significant other in your life. *(25 minutes)*
13. *Homework:* Write a draft narrative about a significant other in your life and how the incident reveals character.

DAY 5

POSTREADING ACTIVITIES (CONT'D)

14. *Peer-edit student essays:* Have students read each other's essays and use 6+1 traits to offer specific feedback. *(25 minutes)*
15. *Oral presentation (optional):* Volunteers present their essays orally. *(30 minutes)*

Now consider a very different SRE for a very different text. Suppose a similar class is reading a simple and straightforward narrative, something like Bret Harte's "The Outcast of Poker Flats (Harte, 1960)." Suppose further that your goals for having students read the story are simply to appreciate and enjoy this entertaining tale and briefly review the literary elements of setting, characterization, conflict, and theme. In this case, the SRE outlined in the following figure, which spans only two days and includes only six activities, would be appropriate, because the students, the story itself, and the purpose for reading the story do not require a longer and more supportive SRE.

SRE Supporting Bret Harte's "The Outcast of Poker Flats"

DAY 1
PREREADING ACTIVITIES

1. *Motivating:* Discuss which figures in literature students have previously read might considered "improper persons" worthy of banishment. *(10 minutes)*
2. *Building background knowledge:* Provide brief information on Harte and the setting of the story. *(5 minutes)*

DURING-READING ACTIVITY (HOMEWORK)

3. Have students read the story, making notes on its setting, characterization, climax and theme.

DAY 2
POSTREADING ACTIVITIES

4. *Small-group discussion:* Form small groups to focus on each of the four literacy elements being reviewed. *(15 minutes)*
5. *Whole-class discussion:* Consider all four of the leterary elements the small groups dealt with. *(15 minutes)*
6. *Writing:* Outline a somewhat similar story but with a different setting, main character, climax, and theme. *(20 minutes)*

Critical Constructs Underlying Scaffolded Reading Experiences

A substantial body of theory and research, described thoroughly in Graves and Graves (2003) and Fitzgerald and Graves (2004), underlies the SRE approach. Below we highlight four of the most important underlying constructs. (We have already introduced two of these concepts—*scaffolding* and the *zone of proximal development,* but we want to say a bit more about each of them.)

Scaffolding can also help students better complete a task, complete a task with less stress or in less time, or learn more fully.

Scaffolding

Scaffolding (Clark and Graves 2005; Wood, Bruner, and Ross 1976) is at the heart of this approach. In the preface we defined a scaffold as a temporary supportive structure that enables a child to successfully complete a task he or she could not complete without the aid of the scaffold. Here, we modify that definition in an important way by adding that scaffolding can also help students better complete a task, complete a task with less stress or in less time, or learn more fully. An SRE maximizes the chances that students will understand the reading, learn from it, and generally enjoy and profit from both what they read and the experience of reading it.

The Zone of Proximal Development

The zone of proximal development (Vygotsky 1978) is a concept very closely related to that of scaffolding. The notion calls attention to the social nature of learning and emphasizes that at any particular time, students have a circum-scribed zone of development, a range within which they can learn. At one end of this range are learning tasks they can complete independently; at the other end are learning tasks they cannot complete, even with assistance. In between these two extremes is the zone most productive for learning, the range of tasks at which students can succeed *if* they are assisted by some more knowledge-able or more competent other. This, of course, is the zone in which we want students to be working, and one major purpose of SREs is to put learners in this zone.

The Gradual Release of Responsibility

The gradual release of responsibility model (Pearson and Gallagher 1983) is another important concept behind SREs. As shown in the next figure, the model depicts a progression in which students gradually move from situations in which the teacher takes the majority of the responsibility for their success-fully completing a task (in other words, does most of the work for them) to situations in which students assume increasing responsibility for the task and finally to situations in which students take total or nearly total responsibility for the task.

Unfortunately, in practice the "gradual" feature of the model is frequently truncated. We all too frequently introduce a topic or concept and then proceed as though students have mastered it immediately. Immediate mastery is rare. Learning takes time, time during which students need our continued support. As students move beyond the elementary grades, our continued support tends to get even less frequent. The thinking is that older students are nearing maturity and therefore ought to become increasingly independent, and that is certainly the case as far as it goes. However, middle school and high school students are asked to do increasingly complex tasks with increasingly challenging texts. They need continued support with these more challenging texts and tasks at the same time that we gradually withdraw support from less challenging texts and tasks.

The Gradual Release of Responsibility Model

PROPORTION OF RESPONSIBILITY FOR READING EXPERIENCE

| All Teacher | Joint Responsibility | All Student |

| Modeling and Instruction | Guided Practice / Gradual Release of Responsibility | Practice and Application |

Experiencing Success

The final construct we discuss here is that of success. A dominant thought motivating the SRE approach is the overwhelming importance of success. As the professional judgments of both teachers and research have repeatedly verified (Guthrie and Wigfield 2000; Malloy, Marinak, and Gambrell 2010; Pressley 2006), if students are going to learn to read effectively, they need to succeed at the vast majority of reading tasks they undertake. Moreover, if students are going to become not only proficient readers but also avid readers—students, and later adults, who voluntarily read for information, enjoyment, and personal fulfillment—then successful reading experiences are even more important. There are several ways in which reading experiences can be successful:

1. Most important, reading is successful when the reader understands what he or she has read.

2. Reading is successful when the reader finds it enjoyable, entertaining, in-formative, or thought-provoking. Not every reading experience will yield all these benefits, but every experience should yield at least one of them.

3. Reading is successful when it prepares the reader to complete whatever task follows the reading.

To a great extent, children's success in reading is directly under your control as a teacher. You can select (and allow your students to select) materials they can read. To the extent the material they read presents challenges, you can provide support before, during, and after they read that will enable them to meet those challenges. Additionally, you can select and help them select postreading activities they can complete successfully.

However, there is an extremely important qualification. Saying students should succeed at the reading tasks you ask them to complete and that you should do everything possible to ensure success does not mean spoon-feeding them. Unless readers undertake some challenging tasks, unless they are willing to take some risks and make some attempts they are not certain of and get feedback on their efforts, there is little room for learning to take place. Moreover, as Csikszentmihalyi (1990) discovered in more than four decades of research, facing significant challenges and meeting them is one of the most fulfilling and rewarding experiences a person can have. In order to develop as readers, children need challenges. However, it is vital that teachers arrange and scaffold reading activities so that students can meet these challenges.

Differentiating Instruction

Helping all students be successful in their reading while at the same time challenging them sufficiently are excellent maxims for teaching. However, not all students are equally skilled. Sometimes you need to provide readers with different support and different reading tasks. At the same time, this differentiation cannot take a huge amount of your time, should not stigmatize an individual or group, and must produce results. One way to do this is to provide a basic set of SRE experiences to all students, provide additional scaffolding for students who need it, and provide additional reading or writing activities for students who don't.

Sometimes you need to provide readers with different support and different reading tasks.

Suppose a class of thirty-five seniors is going to read *The Night Thoreau Spent in Jail,* Jerome Lawrence and Robert E. Lee's 1972 play drawing a parallel between Thoreau's refusing to pay taxes to support the Mexican-American War and protests over the Vietnam War. Thirty students are able readers and can handle the play and some additional reading. Five students, however, will need help with the play. In this situation we might create a set of SRE activities that all students will complete, prepare some additional SRE activities to support the less skilled readers, assign some additional reading to the more skilled readers while we are working with the less skilled readers, and offer options for postreading activities to accommodate both groups.

Here is a list of the prereading and during-reading activities for all students, additional prereading and during-reading activities to support your less skilled readers in small caps, additional reading for your more skilled readers to do while you are working with the less skilled ones, and options for postreading activities.

SRE SUPPORTING JEROME LAWRENCE AND ROBERT E. LEE'S *THE NIGHT THOREAU SPENT IN JAIL*

PREREADING ACTIVITIES

1. *Building Background Knowledge:* About Thoreau, the Mexican-American War, and the Vietnam War.

2. *PRETEACHING VOCABULARY AND CONCEPTS:* THERE ARE SEVERAL CONCEPTS AND SOME CHALLENGING VOCABULARY THAT SOME READERS WILL NEED HELP WITH.

3. *BUILDING TEXT-SPECIFIC KNOWLEDGE:* EXPLAINING THE TIME AND SETTING SHIFTS THAT MAY CONFUSE SOME READERS.

(continues)

(continued)

ADDITIONAL READING FOR MORE SKILLED READERS

4. *Silent Reading:* Able readers read "Civil Disobedience" on their own with the understanding that they will be considering how well Thoreau's thinking is represented in *The Night Thoreau Spent in Jail.*

DURING-READING ACTIVITIES

5. *Silent Reading:* Your better readers will read Act 1 independently.
6. *READING TO STUDENTS:* YOU READ ACT 1 ALOUD TO THE LESS SKILLED READERS.
7. *Oral Reading by Students:* Students will take parts and read Act II as a whole-class activity.

POSTREADING OPTIONS

8. *Graphic Activity:* Students search editorials and commentaries from newspapers and magazines of the Vietnam era and create a display representing the opinions of the time. They may wish to annotate their displays with their own comments.
9. *Outreach Activity:* Students interview adults who were alive during the Vietnam era and write an essay comparing their attitudes to those depicted in the play.
10. *Writing:* Students write an essay in which they consider how well the play represented the ideas Thoreau presented in "Civil Disobedience."

This of course is only one way in which SREs can be used to differentiate activities, but it does illustrate an attempt to give some students additional support, not separate students any more than necessary, not differentiate any more than necessary, and provide additional activities for the larger group while working with the smaller one.

A Final Word

In this chapter, we have explained just what an SRE is. In doing so, we have discussed the purpose of SREs, described the SRE framework, listed the components of SREs, briefly described each of them, emphasized that individual SREs will vary markedly, described some important constructs underlying the SRE approach, and discussed differentiating SREs. The next chapter discusses and gives examples of prereading activities.

CHAPTER 1

Prereading Activities

Mr. Johnson is preparing his tenth-grade American literature students to read Alice Walker's "Everyday Use," a story in which an heirloom quilt becomes the focus of a struggle between cultural identity and family harmony for a mother and her two very different daughters. Mr. Johnson knows how important it is, as he says, "to prime my students when they read a story. They often don't do their best when they jump in cold."

The students in Mr. Johnson's second-hour class have assembled in pairs. As requested, they have each brought from home an everyday object, something that has some significance to them and to at least one other family member. The array of objects is astonishing, as varied as the members of the class. Jenny has brought her grandmother's locket; Jeff, his uncle's dented trumpet. Margo has brought an armless doll, and Bob has a Grateful Dead T-shirt. Much to Mr. Johnson's secret delight, Annie has dragged in a homemade quilt. Mr. Johnson asks the pairs of students to talk about the significance of the object, why they chose it, and what it might mean to other members of the family. At the end of an animated twenty minutes of explaining and sharing,

Mr. Johnson says, "We've seen how everyday objects can mean different things to different family members. Let's see how this plays out in the story we'll read for tomorrow, 'Everyday Use,' by Alice Walker."

That students should succeed in all the reading experiences they undertake is one of the central principles motivating the SRE approach. And the first opportunity you have to start students on the road to a successful reading experience is at the beginning. Prereading activities, the initial set of activities in an SRE, prepare students to read, making sure they get off to a good start. Taking time to prepare students before they read will pay big dividends in terms of their understanding what they read, learning from what they read, and finding the reading an enjoyable and rewarding experience.

Taking time to prepare students before they read will pay big dividends in terms of their understanding what they read.

The ten categories of prereading activities serve five different purposes:

1. *Motivating and relating the reading to students' lives* activities get students interested and enthusiastic about reading the selection.

2. *Building or activating background knowledge, providing text-specific knowledge, preteaching vocabulary,* and *preteaching concepts* activities give them information they need to understand the text.

3. *Prequestioning, predicting, and setting direction* activities alert students about what they should attend to as they read.

4. *Suggesting strategies* activities remind students of strategies they already know that will be particularly useful in reading the selection.

5. *Considering literary elements* and *suggesting literary lenses* activities deal directly with literary concerns.

As you choose and design activities, you'll find that many of them overlap. That's fine. We created the categories to suggest the range of options available, not because you need to classify each activity you create as this or that. What's important is that the activities you choose assist your students in achieving the purposes you and they have for reading a particular selection.

In planning an SRE you first consider three factors—the students, the selection, and the purpose(s) for which students are reading. After either you or your students have selected the text to read and after you have read through it and identified topics, themes, potential difficulties, and other relevant features of the material, you map out the entire SRE. The following questions inform the activity categories from which you select:

- **What is your students' overall goal for reading—is it primarily for an aesthetic experience, or is it to gain information or insights?**
- **Will getting the gist of the material be sufficient, or do students need to gain a deep and thorough understanding?**

As you continue planning an effective SRE, ask:

- **How can I get these students really interested in this selection?**
- **What background knowledge do they have on this topic?**
- **What might they need to know to profit most from their reading?**
- **Is there anything in the material that I can relate to their lives?**
- **Are there any concepts or vocabulary in the selection that students might benefit from working with beforehand?**
- **Could they use any of their repertoire of reading strategies to help them better understand the material?**
- **What literary elements is this selection best suited to showcase?**
- **Does a particular literary lens (a topic we discuss in Chapter 4) shed light on understanding and responding to this selection?**

The sample activities in this book all follow the same format. Each begins with a heading identifying the type of activity and naming it. Underneath there may be a sentence or two describing the activity. Next come sections on the selection, the students for whom the activity was written, the reading purpose(s), the goal(s) of the activity, the procedure to follow, and other selections with which you might use the activity. In the final section, reflections, we (as informally as one can in a printed book) expand on ideas and issues related to the activity. Most of the time, we comment on the activity itself—what it did, what it did not do, how it might be changed, and the like. Less frequently, we comment on a general principle the activity brings to mind. We hope these informal reflections encourage your own reflections.

PREREADING ACTIVITIES IN THIS CHAPTER

Motivating

A big part of preparing students to read is motivating them. Whatever the task, it is always more interesting, exciting, and meaningful if we have a good reason for wanting to do it. Think about yourself and your own reading. Why do you pick up the evening newspaper, seek out an article in the *English Journal*, or read a mystery novel? Is there a particular purpose you have in mind? Do you read to be informed, enlightened, inspired, entertained? We all read for a combination of reasons, but they usually stem from our expectation that the text will give us something we need or want—information, inspiration, entertainment, whatever. In order to ensure a successful reading experience, we need to make certain students have this sort of motivation.

You know what kinds of things interest and excite your students. Use these to help motivate their reading.

Motivational activities are just that—activities that incite enthusiasm, an eagerness to delve into the material. Some activities are solely motivational. However, motivational activities frequently overlap with other kinds of prereading activities—particularly activating background knowledge and relating reading to students' lives. In general, motivational activities draw on the interests and concerns of the particular group doing the reading. A rap might be part of a motivating activity for younger adolescents, while a contemporary issue might pique the interest of high school students. You know what kinds of things interest and excite your students. Use these to help motivate their reading.

Motivational activities often feature "hands-on" experiences, active student participation, dramatization, and questions that intrigue. For example:

- **Have you ever had a really disappointing birthday even though you were looking forward to it?**
- **Why do people who seem so different become fast friends? Are you and your best friend more different than alike?**
- **What kind of stuff do you carry around in your backpack? What do those things say about you?**
- **Think about a time when you did something you knew you weren't supposed to. How did you feel afterward? What lesson did you learn?**

Once students' interest is piqued, the next step is to transfer that interest to the reading material. Consider these follow-ups to the questions above:

- **In the story "Eleven," by Sandra Cisneros (1991), a teacher ruins a young girl's special day.**
- **The two protagonists of *Of Mice and Men*, George and Lenny, are about as different as night and day.**

- What do the contents of a backpack say about a soldier? That's what Tim O'Brien tackles in his Vietnam story, *The Things They Carried*.

- Gary Soto has a unique take on what it feels like to do something wrong in his short story "The Pie."

Here, we present a sample motivating activity for an intriguing short story.

MOTIVATING—Words to Ponder

Words to Ponder motivates students, guides them, and gives them opportunities to interact as they consider a challenging and disturbing proposition.

Selection: "House Taken Over," by Julio Cortazar. As is typical of Cortazar's short stories, this one begins in the real world, then moves toward fantasy, inviting students to connect the familiar—a brother, a sister, and an ancestral home—before delving into the ambiguous and uncertain. The themes—the necessity of thinking and the fear of encountering the unknown— are ones many adolescent face. This story casts these personal issues into the public sphere.

Students: High school students of various abilities.

Reading Purposes: To deeply understand a complex story and to relate some of its themes to one's own life.

Goal of the Activity: To get students deeply involved in one of the central issues of the story.

Procedure:

- Project this quotation on an overhead, LCD, or interactive whiteboard: ". . . and little by little we stopped thinking. You can live without thinking" (Cortazar 1944).

- Ask students to explain three things in a journal entry. *First, do you agree or disagree with this statement? Second, what do you think the statement means? Finally, give a real-world example: how does it support your position?* Their response should be at least a full page.

- Ask students who agreed with the statement to move to one side of the classroom, those who disagreed to the other side. Give each group five minutes to clarify with one another what they think the statement means. They should be ready to share with the class one carefully crafted explanation of what the statement means, as well as three or four examples.

- Have a spokesperson for each group present that group's explanation. Then have several students present their examples. Lead a lively discussion of the value of thinking and how essential students think it is. Some students may have read *1984, Brave New World, The Giver*, or other dystopian novels. They may want to discuss the connections between those texts (the repression of an individual's freedom to think) and this quote.

(continues)

(continued)

Other Selections: This activity can be used with any selection that includes a pithy theme students can connect to another work they have read. A close reading of Robert Burns' poem "To a Mouse" can help students uncover the significance of Steinbeck's *Of Mice and Men.* Tolstoy's comment in *Anna Karenina*—"Happy families are all alike. Every unhappy family is unhappy in its own way"—can trigger a discussion of any literary work that has family dynamics at its heart, including *Death of a Salesman, Fences,* and *A Doll's House.* The statement in *To Kill a Mockingbird* that "you never really understand a person until you consider things from his point of view—until you climb into his skin and walk around in it" is a unifying theme for any literary work that asks students to consider things from someone else's perspectives.

Reflections: *In addition to motivating students to want to read the story, this activity activates student' background knowledge about one of its themes. Motivational activities often accomplish some goal beyond motivating students, and that's great. But remember that doing something solely for the sake of motivating students is well worthwhile. Meeting an additional goal is a bonus. Also, a little warning: what students need to get interested and actively involved is ideas that will help them as they read. Motivating activities need to direct students' attention to the themes, topics, and concepts in the reading. You're not just trying to get students interested and excited, you're trying to get them interested and excited in the particular selection.*

Relating the Reading to Students' Lives

Relating the reading to their lives is a powerful way to get students to commit themselves to a text, to own it. When we see how something relates to our lives, we make a personal connection—we have a vested interest.

Suppose your class of tenth graders includes a number of Somali students. You also have copies of "When Mr. Pirzada Came to Dine," one of the short stories in Jhumpa Lahiri's Pulitzer Prize–winning collection, *Interpreter of Maladies.* Helping your Somali students relate to the story is easy. Like the young protagonist, they are far from their homeland, which has been torn by war, and they are trying to adjust in a new world. But what about your non-Somali students, students born and raised in the United States, most of them in fact born and raised in the city where you teach? A discussion topic that may help them to relate: *what could they do to help students new to the United States feel more comfortable in their new setting?* If you choose to push the matter a bit, you might ask them to write about some things they could have done to help new immigrants but did not.

Relating the reading to students' lives includes any activities that help students understand how what they read has meaning for the world they live in, just one of which is exemplified here.

RELATING THE READING TO STUDENTS' LIVES—Ownership

Ownership helps bridge the gap between themes or other aspects of a story and students' experiences by asking them to explore a concept central to the story and central to their own lives or things they care about.

Selection: "Independence," by Ruth Sasaki. The story opens in 1964, when two Japanese American sisters, Cathy and Sharon, get a summer job at a Lake Tahoe cabin in order to experience life without constant parental supervision. Cathy and Sharon begin the job with high expectations but struggle in their new position for just three weeks and then ask to return home. The story is a relatively easy read but addresses numerous themes that can trigger great discussion, like the price of becoming independent and the ramifications of being Japanese American. Sasaki's skillful narration includes subtle details and has a distinctive tone. It's a wonderful story about growing up, looking back, and taking responsibility.

Students: Middle school students of mixed abilities.

Reading Purpose: To enjoy an interesting and informative work of fiction that deals with a theme important to many teens.

Goal of the Activity: To bridge the gap between readers' lives and those of the story's main characters by exploring a theme central to both the story and their lives—independence.

Procedure:

- Write the word *independence* on the board and ask students to define it. Have them provide examples of independence; encourage them to consider both personal independence and the independence nations have.

- Have students take out their reading journals or notebooks, set up a page with two columns—the advantages of independence and the disadvantages of independence—and enter as many of each as they can. Then, underneath the columns, ask them to write about a time they felt independent.

- After they have finished writing, have them, in pairs, discuss (for about five minutes) their lists, and select the strongest three or four advantages of independence and the strongest three or four disadvantages of independence.

- Reconvene the class and ask for volunteers to write their answers on the board. Then lead a discussion about the advantages and disadvantageous of independence.

Others Selections: This activity can be used with any novel, story, or biography that has a central theme students can relate to. A few include Harper Lee's *To Kill a Mockingbird* (prejudice), Sherman Alexie's short stories (the importance of humor when one grows up as a member of a marginalized community), and *The Diary of Anne Frank* (the triumph of optimism over despair).

(continues)

(continued)

Reflections: *Some students will ramble when writing about and discussing ideas like indepen-dence, so it's a good idea to circulate and keep them on track. Also, you might continue this activity during the other two SRE phases. While they read, students might record instances of Cathy and Sharon's attempts at independence. After they have finished the story, they can discuss what they discovered about adolescents' search for independence. Again, remember the focus of the activity needs to be something in students' lives that is central to the selection. It's of little benefit, for example, to have an extended activity on social networking sites just because a character in a story occasionally uses Facebook.*

Building or Activating Background Knowledge

No text contains all the information necessary to understand it; readers need to fill in what's missing. This requires a huge store of background knowledge. Students come to school knowing a great number of concepts, but they don't all know the same things. Some students have been read to from an early age, read widely on their own, travel to or have lived in other places, take trips to museums, go on nature outings, and belong to groups such as boys' and girls' clubs; they've had a wide variety of experiences. Students from other countries and cultures may have had equally rich experiences but these experiences are not as relevant to those they encounter in much of what they read in school. Still other students have not had the benefit of these kinds of rich experience.

You need to be certain that *all* students have the background knowledge necessary to fully understand, respond to, and enjoy the texts they work with in your classes. This means carefully evaluating the texts and the knowledge they assume, carefully evaluating your students and the knowledge they have, and being sure that those who do not have that knowledge get it.

Sometimes that means *providing* background knowledge, a very different thing from merely *activating* their existing knowledge (Hirsch 2010–11). For example, if your seventh graders are going to read an article on poverty in Appalachia that assumes readers already know quite a bit about Appalachia—where it's located, how populated the area is, what sorts of people live there—you are going to have to teach that information before they read the article.

At other times, students have the relevant information they need but don't realize they have it or don't think about it in a way that brings it to the surface. In these cases, you need to *activate* this prior knowledge with prereading experiences that prompt them to be conscious of it. Students might write about what they know, then talk about it with their classmates. Everyone can then connect this shared information with similar ideas they encounter in the text.

Here, we describe an activity for *building* background knowledge. *Activating* background knowledge is of course less time consuming.

BUILDING BACKGROUND KNOWLEDGE—Places, Events, and Times

This activity *builds* background knowledge. (*Activating* it usually takes less time.)

Selection: *Number the Stars*, by Lois Lowry. In this story, ten-year-old AnnMarie and her family help their neighbors, the Rosens, flee to Sweden in order to escape Nazi persecution.

Students: Sixth and seventh graders of mixed abilities.

Reading Purpose: To understand, enjoy, and appreciate a well-written historical novel.

Goal of the Activity: To explain the geographic and historical setting of the novel so that students can better understand and appreciate the situation faced by the main characters.

Procedure:

- Write *1943*; *Copenhagen, Denmark*; and *Germany* on the board.
- Tell students that something very tragic was happening in Germany in 1943. If students are familiar with the Nazis, Hitler, and the Holocaust, let them discuss what they know.
- If not, briefly explain the situation to them. Tell them that during this time German troops began to "relocate" all the Jews of Denmark—to take them to concentration camps.
- Locate Germany, Denmark, and Copenhagen on a map.
- Tell students that this story takes place in Copenhagen, Denmark, during this period in history. Explain that the main character AnnMarie isn't Jewish, but her best friend Ellen is. You also may want to give some background information on the Jews and the Jewish religion. Explain that because of where and when the Jewish people in the novel lived they faced situations calling for personal sacrifice, daring, and courage.

Other Selections: Giving information on places, events, and time periods before students read a selection is appropriate any time these elements play key roles in a piece and are therefore important to understanding and appreciating the ideas presented. Many selections, fiction as well as nonfiction, revolve around important historical events and figures. A few that require some explanation of context are *The Watsons Go to Birmingham—1963*, *The Diary of Anne Frank*, and *The Red Badge of Courage*.

Reflections: *Although this activity is simple and straightforward, the information will be quite helpful to some students and crucial to others. Sometimes students have little or no knowledge—or may have misconceptions—about the places, events, and time periods in the material they are asked to read. Even those students who do have fairly well developed, accurate views benefit from more information or new insights. Accurate information about places and events can bolster students' enjoyment of historical-based texts, allow them to connect their reading to their knowledge of geography and history, and give them valuable information about the world they live in.*

Providing Text-Specific Knowledge

Students sometimes need information specific to a text. Tenth graders asked to read *All Quiet on the Western Front* will probably have some general knowledge about World War I but will need specific information about what combat was like then. In order to understand and enjoy *The Great Gatsby* fully, students need to know something about the Jazz Age and the American Dream. This kind of information is easily conveyed in a brief prereading discussion of interesting supporting material.

Another way to provide text-specific knowledge is to give students a preview (similar to previews of movies and TV shows) of the material (Chen and Graves 1998; Graves, Prenn, and Cooke 1985). A preview of an article, chapter, or informational book could include the topics, events, people, or places dealt with and unusual or difficult vocabulary. A preview of a novel or short story might introduce the setting, characters, and something about the plot.

The following example presents a fairly substantial preview.

PROVIDING TEXT-SPECIFIC KNOWLEDGE—
The Coming Attraction

The Coming Attraction gives students a substantial preview of a book they are about to read.

Selection: *Fahrenheit 451*, by Ray Bradbury. This classic dystopian novel of a future America in which critical thought is outlawed and books are burned to prevent the spread of "dangerous" ideas continues to be all too relevant today.

Students: High school seniors taking a required English course to graduate.

Reading Purposes: To help understand the rich characters and themes in *Fahrenheit 451*, identify the techniques Ray Bradbury used to create these characters and themes, analyze aspects of the American character depicted in the book's futuristic society, and recognize those same aspects in contemporary American society.

Goal of the Activity: To give students a substantial amount of information about the story in order to make their reading more successful and enjoyable.

Procedure: Read the following preview to students before they read the story:

> Can you imagine a world in which no one is allowed to read? Can you picture a country that outlaws education in an attempt to keep you ignorant and misinformed? Can you envision a society in which you have no individual rights or freedoms? How do you think you would react to an environment of this sort?

This very environment is depicted in Ray Bradbury's novel *Fahrenheit 451*. Set in America during the not-too-distant future, *Fahrenheit 451* follows the adventures of Guy Montag, a firefighter whose job is not to put out fires but to start them. Specifically, Montag and his fellow firefighters burn books, which have been outlawed by the government. If you are caught reading books in this future America, they are burned, perhaps along with more of your possessions; you may even be put to death. Despite this threat, Montag becomes interested in finding out what is so powerful about books and reading, which puts him on a collision course with his overseer, Captain Beatty, and the society in which he lives.

Will Montag's interest in books lead to his death? Will Montag be able to change himself and his society? Is there any hope for this America of tomorrow? These questions will be answered as we read *Fahrenheit 451*.

Other Selections: The major concern when providing a preview is the amount of detail to include; you want to be sure students get just enough but not too much information. That said, previews can be used with virtually any fiction or nonfiction text that you determine your students will find challenging.

Reflections: *The main question with previews is how often to use them. The answer is: just enough but not too much. We all like a little information about something we're about to read but not too much; we don't want to know the punch line of a joke, who committed the murder, or the climax and denouement of a story line. Too much is too much. Still, with challenging texts—novels like* The Giver, *by Lois Lowry, for a sixth grader,* A Lesson Before Dying, *by Ernest J. Gaines, for a ninth grader, and* Beloved, *by Toni Morrison, for a twelfth grader—previews are extremely useful.*

Preteaching Vocabulary

Preteaching vocabulary provides students with the meanings of challenging words before they read a selection so that they can focus on the ideas the author is presenting rather than on unknown words. For example, before sixth graders read the classic short story "Rikki-Tikki-Tavi," by Rudyard Kipling, they need to be familiar with words like *valiant, sluice, providence, cowered,* and *consolation*. When asked to read Tim O'Brien's *The Things They Carried*, many tenth or eleventh graders benefit from being pretaught (among other words) *eviscerate, acquiescence, platitude, reticence, rectitude, salvage,* and *denotation*.

There are any number of vocabulary activities you can engage students in prior to their reading a selection. Here is just one of them.

PRETEACHING VOCABULARY—Word Clues

Word Clues introduces potentially difficult vocabulary using context-rich sentences in teacher-created worksheets.

Selection: "Thomas Nast: Political Cartoonist Extraordinaire," by Lynn Evans. Bavarian-born Thomas Nast is responsible for creating some of our most notable and enduring political symbols—the Republican elephant, the Democratic donkey, and Uncle Sam. The piece chronicles his life from his experiences as a poor student good only at art to his thirty-year partnership with *Harper's Weekly* and his powerful political influence as a cartoonist.

Students: Seventh, eighth, and ninth graders of average to low ability.

Reading Purpose: To understand and recall some of the important highlights of Thomas Nast's life and work.

Goals of the Activity: To introduce potentially difficult vocabulary; let students practice using context clues to unlock word meaning.

Procedure:

- Before the lesson, select five to ten words that are important to understanding this piece and that you suspect some of your students may have trouble reading (like *draftsman*, *emigrated*, *reform*, *endorsed*, *symbol*, *corruption*, and *critical*).

- Present each word in a context-rich sentence or paragraph that provides clues to word's meaning. Following this sentence or paragraph, create two questions that will help students use context clues to unlock the word's meaning. Here is an example for the word *emigrated*:

Thomas Nast emigrated to the United States in 1840 when he was just six years old. He and his mother and sister settled in New York City.

1. **Based on the sentences above, Thomas Nast probably left his home country and came to live in the United States. True or false?**

2. *Emigrated* **probably means:**
   a. **took clothes and food to poor people**
   b. **left one country to settle in another**
   c. **ran a very difficult uphill race**
   d. **borrowed enough money to buy a house**

- Tell students that the selection contains some challenging vocabulary. Pass out the worksheet, guide students through the first item, and let them complete the rest of the items individually or in pairs.

- After students have completed the worksheet, briefly discuss their answers.
- In place of individual worksheets, you could present the material to the whole class using an LCD or interactive white board. Also, you might sometimes let students pick the words to study. After students have completed a number of these worksheets, let them create their own to exchange with a classmate.

Other Selections: This activity can be used with any text that includes challenging vocabulary able to be decoded in context, texts like "A Rose for Emily," by William Faulkner; "The Masque of the Red Death," by Edgar Allan Poe; or "A Very Old Man with Enormous Wings," by Gabriel Garcia Marquez.

Reflections: *This activity takes quite a bit of preparation, and you will probably want to use it primarily with students who need practice using context clues. Then again, using context clues to unlock word meanings is a very useful skill, and many students will profit from becoming more adept at it; you may therefore use it fairly often. Remember, students can create instructional items like these themselves. (And middle and high school students can create vocabulary items of this sort for elementary students.)*

Preteaching Concepts

As we noted in the Introduction, what distinguishes preteaching vocabulary from preteaching concepts is that vocabulary instruction teaches new labels for known concepts, while concept instruction focuses on words that represent new and potentially difficult ideas (Graves 2009). *Subliminal message,* for example, is probably a new concept for eighth graders, and *archetype* might be a new concept for eleventh graders.

Ideally, students will be reading material that contains concepts they can handle comfortably but at the same time provides opportunities to deepen their current knowledge of concepts or learn new ones. For example, most of the concepts in *The Giver*, by Lois Lowry, are familiar to competent eighth or ninth graders, but they might need help with *transgression, independence, anguish,* and *resistance*. The vocabulary of Toni Morrison's *Beloved* is probably within reach of most high school seniors yet offers opportunities to deepen their knowledge of concepts such as *rememory, abolition,* and *stream of consciousness*.

How you introduce concepts to students depends on how familiar they already are with them and how well they need to know them in order to achieve their reading goals. Graves (2006) and Stahl and Nagy (2006) provide additional information on teaching concepts. Here, we describe one way to do so.

PRETEACHING CONCEPTS—Stalwart Instruction

Stalwart Instruction uses a very powerful approach to concept instruction to give students a solid understanding of an important concept.

Selection: "The Man to Send Rain Clouds," by Leslie Marmon Silko. This is the first published work of an accomplished and widely heralded contemporary writer who has Laguna Pueblo, Mexican, and white ancestors. Silko wrote this story while an English major at the University of New Mexico. It earned her a National Endowment for the Humanities Discovery Grant and clearly indicates both her strength as an author and her understanding of *cultural symbiosis*, a concept this activity explores. She later taught creative writing and a course in oral tradition for the English department at UNM.

Students: High school students in a multicultural literature class.

Reading Purposes: To appreciate and understand the elements of a well-crafted short story; become familiar with the work of a major multicultural author; recognize the synthesis of cultures, traditions, and actions that sometimes mark modern United States society; celebrate both one's own and Native American culture.

Goal of the Activity: To help students understand cultural symbiosis and the importance of such symbiosis in contemporary American life.

Procedure: Use the five steps of the Frayer method (Frayer, Frederick, and Klausmeier 1969):

- *Define the concept. Cultural symbiosis* is the intermingling of two or more cultural features or practices, the amalgamation of two cultures.

- *Distinguish the concept from other concepts with which it might be mistaken.* The term *symbiosis* normally refers to the physical world. It describes a relationship between two organisms that are interdependent; each gaining benefit from the other. Here, the meaning is psychological.

- *Provide examples and nonexamples.* Examples: Somali high school girls in the United States who wear a *hijab* along with American clothes such as Levis and tennis shoes. The Ben Israelites, a small community of people in India, who generally follow local customs but follow Jewish dietary laws, practice circumcision, and observe the Sabbath. Nonexamples: Sea anemone who live on hermit crabs, to the benefit of both organisms (physical symbiosis, not cultural symbiosis). A person who likes Italian food and French food (there is no amalgamation).

- *Have students distinguish between examples and nonexamples you present.*
  - ▸ A Japanese-French fusion restaurant (*example*). Irish stew (*nonexample*).
  - ▸ A Protestant family that routinely eats fish on Friday (*example*). An Italian gentleman who enjoys playing bocce ball (*nonexample*).

- *Have students produce their own examples and nonexamples.*

Other Selections: The Frayer method can be used with any selection containing new and difficult concepts, from an excerpt from *Into Thin Air*, by John Krakauer, to the Declaration of Independence, to a poem like "The Naming of Parts," by Henry Reed.

Reflections: *The Frayer method has several noteworthy features. First, it begins with a clear definition of the concept. Second, it takes into account that knowing what something involves is knowing what it is not. Finally, it progresses from the teacher doing all the work (steps 1–3), to the teacher and the students sharing the work (step 4), to the students doing all the work (step 5).*

Prequestioning, Predicting, and Setting Direction

Predicting should often be accompanied by thoughtful discussion of what prompted the predictions and how certain or speculative the predictions are.

While all of the prereading activities we describe in this chapter are designed to be implemented before a student reads a text, the three that we focus on here are specifically designed to point students toward certain aspects of the text. Such prereading activities encourage students to think analytically, critically, and creatively. Because these three activities are so closely related, we will consider them together and suggest a single activity that includes all three of them.

Posing questions before students read a selection gives them something to look for as they read. The questions both direct their attention and prompt them to be active, inquisitive learners.

Predicting activities encourage students to speculate about the text based on various prompts—illustrations, titles or subtitles, key words, character names or descriptions, and short excerpts. After students make their predictions, one of their reading purposes will be to see whether their predictions are accurate. Encouraging students to make predictions not only focuses their attention and gives them a purpose for reading but also models a useful reading strategy, one they can employ on their own with a variety of texts. Of course, the goal is to encourage reasoned predictions based on the information available, not wild guessing. Thus, predicting should often be accompanied by thoughtful discussion of what prompted the predictions and how certain or speculative the predictions are.

Typically you'll set a direction at the end of your prereading activities— offer your final instruction and encouragement—by telling students what to attend to while they read. Sometimes you'll use oral instructions: "Read the story to find out if your predictions are correct." At other times, you'll write on the board, create a chart, or provide a handout that students can reflect on or refer to. As the following example illustrates, direction-setting activities are typically brief and to the point.

PREQUESTIONING, PREDICTING, AND SETTING DIRECTION—Learning to Look Forward

Learning to Look Forward includes prequestioning, predicting, and setting direction with a classic tale that lends itself particularly well to these activities.

Selection: "The Tell-Tale Heart," by Edgar Allan Poe. More than 150 years after its creation, Poe's chilling tale continues to capture the interest of today's students.

Students: Ninth and tenth graders of mixed ability.

Reading Purposes: To become familiar with one of the great masters of the short story, Edgar Allan Poe, and to predict the end of a suspenseful story.

Goals of the Activity: To improve students' ability to predict the ending of the story based on careful reading and to get students to practice focused reading by training their attention on specific elements of the text.

Procedure:

- *Prequestioning*: Ask whether students have heard of Edgar Allan Poe. Ask them if they have ever seen *The Simpsons* episode that featured "The Raven." Read "The Raven" and discuss how it exemplifies Poe's themes of darkness, dread, and loss. Read the first few lines of the story, and ask who the narrator seems to be and to whom he might be speaking. Then begin reading or playing a recording of someone reading the story (there are some excellent recorded readings of this and other Poe stories).

- *Prediction*: Stop reading (or listening) to the story at the sixth paragraph and ask, *Whose heart is the narrator hearing?*

- *Setting direction*: Tell students to keep track of all the noises mentioned in the story and to pay close attention to how the narrator reveals his feelings. *What clues do you have about how the author wants you to feel about the narrator? When were you sure what was going to happen in the story?*

Other Selections: This activity can be used with other Poe stories such as "The Cask of Amontillado" and many suspense stories by other authors. O. Henry stories sometimes work well too, although they are difficult to predict and may frustrate inexperienced readers if prediction is the sole focus of the activity.

Reflections: *These three interrelated strategies help students become active and engaged readers. They also help students become close readers as they search the story for specific textual cues to support their prediction.*

Suggesting Strategies

Over the past two decades, a number of reading comprehension strategies have been identified as valuable for understanding, learning from, and enjoying text (for example, see Graves, Juel, Graves, and Dewitz 2011; National Reading Panel 2000; Pearson, Roehler, Dole, and Duffy 1992; and Pressley 2006). The most frequently recommended strategies are using prior knowledge, asking and answering questions, making inferences, determining what is important, summarizing, imaging, dealing with graphic information, and monitoring comprehension. Teaching students to use reading strategies is an important part of reading instruction and something that is usually taught during the elementary years. Teaching strategies is not a topic we discuss in this book; however, suggesting opportunities for students to use strategies they have already been taught is.

For instance, you might suggest that students use imaging as they read, consciously creating pictures in their heads of the people and events in the story. Or, if students are reading material they need to remember, you might ask them to summarize each paragraph or subtopic. You might also tell them to look for the most important point in each section of an article or the key words in a poem. Because suggesting strategies is such a straightforward activity, the following sample activity is brief.

SUGGESTING STRATEGIES—And the Answer Is?

And the Answer Is? invites students to ask questions of themselves and of their classmates as they read one of the world's greatest plays.

Selection: *Hamlet,* by William Shakespeare. Considered one of Shakespeare's most demanding plays, *Hamlet* continues to intrigue and challenge both students and literary scholars.

Students: Seniors in an AP class in which they study great literature in considerable depth.

Reading Purpose: To comment critically on the play, focusing on what Shakespeare is doing artistically and what literary techniques he is using to create the desired effects.

Goal of the Activity: To remind students that asking questions as they are reading is a very useful strategy and that asking appropriate questions is just as important, perhaps even more important, than answering them.

(continues)

(continued)

Procedure:

- Point out that Shakespeare is one of the most challenging authors, *Hamlet* is one of his more challenging plays, and part of what makes reading Shakespeare challenging is the language he uses, which is both poetic and representative of the language spoken in England some 400 years ago.

- Tell students that when they come across a word, phrase, or sentence they do not fully understand, they should jot it down and pose a question about it. A general question like "What does *felicity* mean?" is okay, but a more specific question—"When Hamlet says, 'Nothing is either good or bad, but thinking makes it so,' does he really mean it? Are we, the audience, expected to trust Hamlet at this point? Does Shakespeare expect us to agree with this relativistic position?"—is better.

- After students have read an act of the play, give them time to share their questions with their study group. Tell them to save questions their group can't answer for a whole-class discussion.

Other Selections. You can remind students to use any already learned strategy with any text that merits using the strategy: considering characterization in *Of Mice and Men*; identifying point of view in *The House on Mango Street*; analyzing the tone of the poem "My Papa's Waltz," by Theodore Roethke; and so on.

Reflections: *All too often students' learning is ephemeral; it lasts a few weeks, a few days, even a few minutes. Suggesting that students use strategies they already know greatly increases the chances that these strategies will be internalized and serve students over time.*

Considering Literary Elements

Literary elements are the basic building blocks of literary understanding and interpretation. Point of view, metaphor, simile, foreshadowing, setting, genre, and all the rest are tools adolescent readers use to understand literature. They are part of what Bruner (1977) once called the spiral curriculum—concepts that reappear in greater complexity as students progress through school. Considering literary elements in a prereading activity lets students see that these are not decontextualized terms to be memorized but rather a natural and necessary dimension of literary understanding. Here is an example with a contemporary poem.

CONSIDERING LITERARY ELEMENTS—Ways to Tell a Story

Ways to Tell a Story gives students an opportunity to some important literary elements and to see how a skilled author uses these elements.

Selection: "The Gift," by Li-Young Lee. Li-Young Lee is a wonderfully accessible contemporary poet. In this poignant narrative poem, he tells how his father gave him the gift of tenderness by removing a splinter from his finger. Even as a young child, he realizes, through his father's actions, that small acts of kindness are invaluable gifts.

Students: Ninth through twelfth graders of mixed abilities.

Reading Purpose: To apply one's knowledge of literary elements to a contemporary poem in order to deepen one's understanding.

Goals of the Activity: To demonstrate the accessibility of much contemporary poetry and show that literary elements can be applied to better understand a text.

Procedure:
- Have students quickwrite about a time when someone did something nice for them.
- Review the literary terms *free verse*, *metaphor*, and *image*.
- Read the poem aloud, paying particular attention to the rhythm and the lack of rhyme.
- Have students underline specific examples of figurative language.
- Have small groups of students retell the story of the poem in no more than four sentences.
- Reconvene the class and compare the prose and poem versions of the story. Focus on how literary elements enhance the poem's narrative.

Other Selections: Lots of poems and short stories showcase literary elements. Poems: "Fog," by Carl Sandburg (extended metaphor); "The Red Wheelbarrow," by William Carlos Williams (imagery); "How to Eat a Poem," by Eve Merriam (figurative language); "We Real Cool," by Gwendolyn Brooks (rhythm). Short stories: "The Gift of the Magi," by O. Henry (theme); "Geraldo No Last Name," by Sandra Cisneros (character); "Everyday Use," by Alice Walker (symbolism).

Reflections: *The powerful narrative in this poem is an excellent basis for contrasting poetry and prose. Its free verse form, strong figurative language, and vivid imagery reinforce students' understanding of these important literary concepts.*

Suggesting Literary Lenses

One of the primary purposes of this book is to bring together what we know about helping kids *read* texts with what we know about helping kids *interpret* texts. As we asserted in the introduction, we believe that classroom teachers should merge these two ways of thinking about approaching literary texts with secondary students. The following strategy, Suggesting Literary Lenses, is one of the clearest examples of this kind of merging.

This strategy is based on Deborah's previous work (Appleman 2010, 2000), which suggests that contemporary literary theories can be offered to secondary students as ways to make meanings from texts. Each theory provides a different lens through which the meaning can be read and interpreted. To use another metaphor, each lens is a different tool that is part of an interpretive toolkit (see Literary Toolkit in Chapter 4, pp. 77–80). In our experience, in diverse classrooms across the country, students of all ability levels have been able to apply these lenses to a variety of texts.

By suggesting literary lenses, we believe your students will become better, smarter readers. The following introductory activity introduces the notion of literary lenses with a familiar fairy tale.

SUGGESTING LITERARY LENSES—Mirror, Mirror On The Wall

Selection: "Snow White and the Seven Dwarfs" (Any print version will do; we used http://www.literaturecollection.com/a/grimm-brothers/549/

Students: Students of mixed abilities in grades 9–12.

Reading Purpose: To introduce the idea of literary lenses with a familiar text.

Goals of the Activity: Demonstrate that even simple, familiar texts can be enriched through the use of literary lenses; to increase students' basic understanding of some literary lenses and to practice applying them.

Procedure:

- First, have students retell the familiar story of "Snow White and the Seven Dwarfs." Remind them that the story did not originate with Disney Studios but with the Brothers Grimm.

- Have students read a thumbnail description of the social class lens, the gender lens, and the reader response lens. (See Literary Toolkit in Chapter 4, pp. 77–80)

- Divide students into three groups, assign them each a lens, and have them paraphrase the primary significance of their lenses.
- Have students read a text version of "Snow White and the Seven Dwarfs" and then consider it from the point of view of their assigned lens. What themes, words, characters, or ideas are brought into sharper relief as one considers the story from that perspective?
- Have students jigsaw into different groups, so that each theory is represented in the new groups. Ask them to share their interpretations with each other.
- Reconvene as a whole class, rereading the story aloud, if time permits, and discuss how each lens reframed the story.

Other Selections: Many other traditional fairy tales lend themselves to a theoried reading, including "Little Red Riding Hood," "Cinderella," "Sleeping Beauty," and "Goldilocks and the Three Bears." Contemporary animated films such as *Shrek* or *Hoodwinked* can also be used as examples of how contemporary theory can be applied to classic children's tales.

Reflections: *It is difficult to move students away from their Disneyized conception of "Snow White," but it is possible to do so, especially with older students. While some students are initially wary of considering something as "babyish" as literary lenses in English class, the pairing with theory works well. Because students do not have to decipher a difficult literary text as part of the exercise, it allows them to focus fully on the application of the literary lenses. Teachers might also be able to introduce the concept of "archetype" as they discuss the classic components and characters that comprise most traditional fairy tales. The "three little pigs" exercise described in Chapter 4 can also serve as an effective introduction to this activity.*

A Final Word

What you do with students before they read a selection is perhaps more important to their comprehension than what you do after they read it. Mr. Johnson demonstrated his understanding of this maxim in preparing his students to read "Everyday Use," and we believe that his is an example we can all follow.

As we said at the beginning of the chapter, prereading activities motivate and prepare students to read. Sometimes, just one brief prereading activity ensures a successful reading experience. Other times, you may want to provide several. As is always the case with SREs, your approach depends on the selection, the overall purpose for reading it (information, enjoyment), your students' strengths and needs, and the activities students will do while and after they read it.

We are often wary of complicated activities; they seem to overshadow the text. The prereading activities described here will not eclipse or replace the text. Prereading activities that have been carefully selected and modified on the basis of text, context, and student ability set the stage for your students to fully understand, interpret, and appreciate the literary texts that are the heart of the language arts classroom.

CHAPTER 2

During-Reading Activities

Lizzie teaches eighth-grade English in a diverse high school located in an inner-ring suburb in the Midwest. Her class is about to read the short novel *Monster*, by Walter Dean Myers. Lizzie spent three days on prereading activities. She built some background knowledge about the juvenile justice system, an important element of the novel. She created a motivating activity around peer pressure that foreshadowed some of the most important themes of the text. She pretaught some vocabulary, knowing that specific legal terms such as *felony*, *stenographer*, and *accomplice* might interfere with students' comprehension. The class read the prologue together and discussed the unusual appearance of the text, which includes stage directions and different kinds of font. Today, they will read the first chapter, listing characters and first impressions. As the hour ends, Lizzie assigns the next two chapters, wondering apprehensively how she can support her students' out-of-class reading. She hates traditional study guides; she worries that they become an end in themselves, driving students to read searching for specific literal responses (Gallagher 2009). Short of physically being with each of her students as they read (she simultaneously shudders and laughs at the thought), she considers ways to support her students as they are reading on their own—to prepare them for it, to guide them through it, and to take them beyond it. This chapter explores several of them.

DURING-READING ACTIVITIES IN THIS CHAPTER

Silent Reading

Silent reading both *should be* and *is* the most frequent during-reading activity (Atwell 2007). The majority of the time, students will be reading by themselves, silently. The other during-reading activities are designed to support students' reading—to prepare them for it, to guide them through it, and to take them beyond it.

Reading to Students

Sometimes it is appropriate for students to have the material read to them. If the material cries out to be heard—because the language is beautiful and inspiring, because students need a good send-off for a lengthy or challenging selection, because the concepts are new and need interpretation—then hearing the words may help students grasp the material so that when and if they read it on their own, it will hold more meaning, pleasure, and interest. Equally important, people love to listen to books; if your local library is anything like ours, two-thirds of the material people reserve is books on tape, CDs, or mini-MP3s rather than printed material.

Reading aloud to your students also provides a strong model of expressive reading. By reading aloud, you can show your enthusiasm for information, ideas, and language. Storyteller and author Bill Martin, Jr., (1992) has said, "A blessed thing happened to me as a child. I had a teacher who read to me." Jim Trelease

(2001), another prominent proponent of reading aloud, observes that "a large part of the educational research and practice of the last twenty years confirms conclusively that the best way to raise a reader is to read to that child—in the home and in the classroom." Trelease continues, "This simple, uncomplicated fifteen-minute-a-day exercise is not only one of the greatest intellectual gifts you can give a child; it is also the cheapest way to ensure the longevity of a culture." We emphatically agree. Moreover, it is not just children who enjoy being read to and profit from the experience—students of all ages, as well as adults, do, too. Reading to students builds their vocabulary, their knowledge of the world, their knowledge of books and book conventions, and—probably most important—their interest in reading.

Reading aloud to students is one way to demonstrate the beauty and power of language; and for students who struggle with reading on their own or have had little exposure to books, it may be the most significant way (Appleman 2007). The activity that follows demonstrates the power of reading aloud to students, regardless of their grade or reading ability.

READING TO STUDENTS—Verbal Highlighting

Verbal Highlighting demonstrates the power of reading aloud, regardless of students' grade level or reading ability. In it, reading aloud, by both teacher and students, is used to introduce the selection and call attention to key passages.

Selection: "The Pie," by Gary Soto. This short essay by this widely read short story writer, novelist, and poet is a delightful childhood memory filled with vivid description and figurative language.

Students: Seventh through tenth graders of mixed ability.

Reading Purposes: To engage students in a nonfiction text and to help them consider an expository text as a literary experience.

Goals of the Activity: To help students identify significant passages of a text. To offer students an opportunity both to listen carefully as a text is being read aloud and to create a group interpretation as a class.

Procedure:

- Distribute a copy of the essay to each student, along with a colored highlighter.
- Tell students to listen carefully as you read the piece aloud and highlight any passage that seems particularly interesting or significant.

(continues)

(continued)

- Read the entire story aloud.
- Read the selection again. This time, tell students that whenever you come to a passage they have highlighted they should read that passage aloud along with you. (Several students will join you on most passages; almost all of them will join in on the most significant ones.)
- Have students identify which passages most of them found significant and discuss the importance of these passages to understanding the essay.

Other Selections: This activity can be used with both fiction and nonfiction. The texts should be short, since they will be read twice. "Eleven," by Sandra Cisneros; "Seventh Grade," by Lynda Barry; and "The Gift," by Li-Young Li would all be excellent choices.

Reflections: *This activity works well with a variety of genres—fiction, nonfiction, poetry. Students enjoy highlighting passages orally and have excellent follow-up discussions about their common choices. The activity is appropriate for students of all grades but is particularly useful for showing younger students that identifying important passages is a critical component of literary interpretation.*

Supported reading means just that— supporting the thought processes that accompany reading.

Supported Reading

Much of the time, particularly with narratives, students will read the material from beginning to end without stopping to record or reflect on what they are reading. The interactions that take place are often personal ones between the reader and the text. As Rosenblatt (1978) has explained, the primary concern with narratives is likely to be with what happens to students as they read rather than what they remember afterward. Responses to what they have read might be shared after they have read, or perhaps not at all. Sometimes, however, it is appropriate to guide students' reading, to help them focus on, understand, and learn from certain aspects of the text. Supported reading means just that— supporting the thought processes that accompany reading. Supported reading activities can make the reading experience a more positive one for students, assist students in achieving the deep and lasting understanding critical in today's world, and lead students to make connections among ideas in the text and between their existing experience and knowledge with what is presented in the text. All students need support for their reading at some points, but supported reading can be particularly important for struggling readers and for English language learners (Goldenberg 2011).

Although supported reading activities are by no means always needed with narratives, they can be very useful. Perhaps you feel your students would understand and enjoy a story more if they focused their attention on certain aspects of character, setting, plot, or theme. Or maybe you want them to be aware of colorful or unusual language. Maybe you would like for them to make personal responses to what they read, make predictions, or consider how they or the characters are feeling. These are all good reasons for designing supported reading activities.

While useful with narratives, supported reading activities are most frequently used to help students understand and remember the information presented in expository materials. Some general kinds of supported reading activities for expository texts might include:

- **having students focus on various organizational patterns of text such as sequencing, cause and effect, or comparison/contrast**
- **encouraging critical thinking by having students note examples of fact and opinion, make inferences, draw conclusions, or predict outcomes**
- **having students monitor their understanding of what they read**

As with any SRE activities, the value and effectiveness of supported reading will depend on your students, the material they are reading, and the purposes for reading it. What supported reading should do is get students thinking about and manipulating the ideas and concepts in the material in a way that will help them understand, enjoy, and remember it better. The sample activity below is designed to do just that.

SUPPORTED READING—Problem, Solution, Change

In *Problems, Solution, Change,* students record in their journal what they feel to be any *problems* the main character faces, *solutions* to those problems, and *changes* that took place in the main character because of the problem and solution.

Selection: *The True Confessions of Charlotte Doyle,* by Avi. This historical novel is a gripping account of intrigue and murder on the high seas told by a thirteen-year-old girl who finds herself the lone passenger on a sailing ship bound from England to America in 1832. Because of the unusual situation Charlotte finds herself in and the demands it places on her physically, mentally, and emotionally, she goes through a metamorphosis, from a prim and proper school girl to a seasoned sailor who runs away to crew on a sailing ship.

Students: Sixth and seventh graders of mixed abilities.

Reading Purpose: To enjoy an exciting adventure story by focusing on the basic plot elements of problem, solution, and change.

Goals of the Activity: To focus students' attention on the elements of plot as they develop and unfold throughout the novel and to encourage students to make connections between ideas in the text and their knowledge of the world.

(continues)

(continued)

Procedure:

- Read the prologue, "An Important Warning," aloud. It begins, "Not every thirteen-year-old girl is accused of murder, brought to trial and found guilty." The narrator, Charlotte, warns us that "if strong ideas and action offend you, read no more. For my part I intend to tell the truth as *I* lived it." We learn that she begins her adventure as a proper young lady about to embark on a voyage from England to America. We are also forewarned that the trip changes her drastically and that keeping a journal is what enables her to relate "in perfect detail everything that transpired during that fateful voyage across the Atlantic Ocean in the summer of 1832."

- Explain that part of the pleasure and purpose of reading literature is to experience adventures and make discoveries through the actions and thoughts of the main characters. In most fiction they read, students encounter a character faced with a problem. In this adventure-packed novel Charlotte is faced with many difficult problems she must solve on her own. In dealing with each dilemma she is changed just a bit, until by the end of the novel she is a very different person.

- Tell them that as they read the novel they will keep a journal describing Charlotte's problems, solutions, and changes, just as Charlotte did. Keeping track of what happens to Charlotte will extend and enrich their own knowledge; they will explore new ideas along with her. Give each student several sheets of lined paper, and have them fold the paper in thirds to form three columns, with these headings:

  Problem   Solution   How Changed?

- Have them bind the pages in some way—a simple staple will do. You might also provide front and back construction-paper covers they can embellish later.

- Remind students that there are no right or wrong responses. They should record anything they feel is a problem, solution, or change. Sometimes a problem may not have an immediate solution, or a change may not be recognizable at the moment. They may need to read further in the novel to discover solutions and changes; some problems may not be resolved.

- Have students begin reading the novel and keeping their journal. Tell them that when they finish they will have an opportunity to share what they discover about Charlotte and her adventures.

Other Selections: This activity is appropriate for any novel or short story in which the main character has problems to solve or obstacles to overcome. Examples include relatively easy selections like Gary Paulsen's *Hatchet* and William Wu's "Black Powder," as well as more challenging ones like F. Scott Fitzgerald's *The Great Gatsby* and Ignatia Broker's *Night Flying Woman*.

Reflections: *The activity itself takes place while students are reading, but it extends over all three SRE phases. You introduce the activity and explain how to keep the journal before students read the story, they create the journal while they are reading, and they discuss what they have learned when they finish.*

Traditional Study Activities

Traditional study activities share some features with supported reading and could be considered a type of supported reading. They are distinguished here both to highlight the differences and to emphasize the value of each separately. Supported reading activities require a lot of scaffolding. For example, in the *Problem, Solution, Change* activity you (1) explain that novels often focus on characters who face problems, come up with solutions to them, and change in the process; (2) show students how to construct a three-column journal; and (3) model how to complete journal entries. Traditional study activities—highlighting, underlining, taking marginal and other kinds of notes, and summarizing—require much less scaffolding. Often you simply suggest that students highlight, underline, take notes, whatever.

Summarizing is the most mentally demanding—and the most time consuming—and produces the best results.

Most classrooms profit from a combination of more supportive and less supportive during-reading activities. Students sometimes need to be more independent, sometimes less so; and the time you have for creating really supportive activities is limited.

Some caveats about traditional study activities.

First, text can be marked—whether by highlighting, underlining, or taking marginal notes—only if students have their own copy of the material, and often they do not.

Second, the more mental the work students do, the more they gain. Highlighting and underlining do not take much mental effort—or much time for that matter—and therefore are often not that effective. Note taking, whether in the margins or elsewhere, takes a good deal more mental effort—and if done thoughtfully, a good deal more time—and is usually more beneficial. Summarizing is the most mentally demanding—and the most time consuming—and produces the best results.

Then, too, many students need to be taught how to underline, take notes, and summarize effectively. The direct explanation model (Duke and Pearson 2002) is a very powerful approach for doing so. It has five components:

1. An explicit description of the strategy and when and how it should be used.
2. Teacher and/or student modeling of the strategy in action.
3. Collaborative use of the strategy in action.
4. Guided practice using the strategy with gradual release of responsibility.
5. Independent use of the strategy.

Well prepared with this sort of instruction, students will be able to successfully carry out traditional study strategies, such as the summarizing in activity shown in this example.

TRADITIONAL STUDY ACTIVITIES—Chaucer's Tales

In *Chaucer's Tales*, groups of two, three, or four students each read and summarize one of these famous tales and share their summary with the class.

Selection: *The Canterbury Tales*, by Geoffrey Chaucer. *The Canterbury Tales*, written at the end of the fourteenth century, is a landmark of English literature, the earliest English vernacular poetry we know. Although a real challenge in the original, Middle-English version, modern translations make it accessible, if still challenging, for today's students.

Reading Purpose: To give students some knowledge of some of the better known tales.

Goal of the Activity: To familiarize all students with Chaucer's work even though each student has to read only one of the tales.

Procedure:

- Divide students into the same number of groups as the number of tales you want students to become familiar with.

- Assign each group a tale (or let them choose one) and specify requirements for the summary and presentation. (Keep the summaries and the presentations fairly brief. We suggest limiting the reports of two typed pages and the presentations to about ten minutes.)

- Whether students read the tales in or out of class is up to you, but have the groups prepare their summaries in class.

Other Selections: Although some texts are easier to summarize than others and narratives are generally easier to summarize than exposition, almost any text can be summarized, so the possibilities are endless. However, if the purpose of the activity remains the same—each of several groups summarizes and presents a summary of a part of a text so that the class as a whole becomes familiar with a text without reading all of it—the text needs to be important for students to know something about and lend itself to this approach. Collections like *Aesop's Fables* and *One Thousand and One Nights* fall into this group. A different sort of summary describing only part of a selection—a summary/preview—is appropriate when you want to entice readers to read all or part of a selection. Middle school students might give summary/previews of the stories from Francisco Jiménez's *The Circuit*, and high school students might give summary/previews of Sandra Cisneros' *The House on Mango Street* or *Woman Hollering Creek and Other Stories* or Tim O'Brien's *The Things They Carried*.

Reflections: *The world moves rapidly—faster and faster with each passing year—and we sometimes have a tendency to value the new and discard the old. Often that is a productive tendency, but sometimes it's not. Many traditional study activities like summarizing became traditional because they worked and filled a need. The best teaching is almost certainly made up of some combination of traditional as well as novel and innovative approaches.*

Student Oral Reading

Having students read aloud achieves some of the same goals that reading *to* students accomplishes—getting students to experiment with and enjoy the sound of language as well as focus on meaning. Additionally, if done in a supportive, nonthreatening way, student read-alouds can spark their interest, increase their enjoyment, improve their fluency, increase their vocabulary, and add to their storehouse of knowledge and concepts (Wilhelm 2008). Reading aloud in school also helps students be more confident and competent when they have to read aloud later in life, at work, in public meetings, and the like.

There are many kinds of oral reading activities you might use in your classroom. Two popular ones are choral reading and readers' theatre. In choral reading, by using high and low voices, different voice combinations, sound effects, movements, gestures, or increasing or decreasing tempo, students combine their voices to convey the meaning of a text. Choral reading requires rehearsal, which increases the chances that students will add words to their vocabulary and improve their fluency. Choral reading has been traditionally used with poetry, but many narratives lend themselves to it as well. Middle-grade students, for example, might enjoy reading aloud the poems in Sharon Creech's *Love That Dog: A Novel* or Robert W. Service's *The Cremation of Sam McGee*.

Readers' theatre, in which students take turns reading text aloud, often assuming roles, is most effective with plays, poetry, and narratives, but it is occasionally appropriate for expository material as well. Students read "fast or slow, loudly or softly, emphasizing certain words or phrases to reading rate, intonation, and emphasis on the meaning-bearing cadences of language to make print come alive" (Hoyt 1992). Seventh graders who are studying U.S. history might do a readers' theatre presentation of Julius Lester's *To Be a Slave*, which chronicles the tragedy of slavery through many eloquent and provocative voices— the slaves themselves and the comments from various newspaper editors of the time.

Choral reading and readers' theatre are entertaining, cooperative, nonthreatening ways in which students can build meaning from text and learn more about language—its purpose, beauty, and power. They are outlets for oral interpretation and opportunities to perform, to gain confidence in speaking and reading.

Text can also be read aloud in conjunction with what Hoyt (1992) calls "oral interactions" in response to the ideas and information students discover as they read. As students read silently, they mark "hot spots"—ideas they like, don't understand, or disagree with or passages that answer a question they have

Reading aloud in school also helps students be more confident and competent when they have to read aloud later in life.

or that the teacher has posed. In pairs or groups, students then read these "hot spots" aloud and talk about them.

Choral reading, readers theatre, and oral interactions are only three of many kinds of oral reading activities you might use in your classroom. Here, we give an example of one of them.

STUDENT ORAL READING—Say It Loud, Say It Proud

In *Say It Loud, Say It Proud,* groups of students determine the meaning of a poem and communicate that meaning by performing an oral interpretation for the rest of the class.

Selections: "Mother to Son" and "I Too Sing America," by Langston Hughes; "Oranges," by Gary Soto; and "Nikki-Rosa," by Nikki Giovanni. These well-known and very accessible poems, by black writers, are each written from a particular speaker's perspective and deliver their message in clear and direct language.

Students: Tenth graders of mixed abilities in an American literature course.

Reading Purposes: To help students create meaning in poetry through oral interpretation and to distinguish between the poet and the speaker of a poem.

Goals of the Activity: To have students create an oral interpretation of a poem and to give them an opportunity to work collaboratively and come to a group interpretation of a literary text.

Procedure: Divide the class into groups of four. Give each group a copy of one of the poems and a sheet of directions. The directions instruct them to read the poem aloud together and come up with an oral interpretation that requires each group member to have an equal speaking part.

- Give each group approximately twenty minutes to create their interpretation.
- Have each group present its interpretation to the whole class, with an introduction that explains why they made the interpretive choices they did.
- Finally, ask each student to write a brief response paper to all of the poem presentations as well as to the process of creating a group oral interpretation for a poem.

Other Selections: This activity can be adapted with short pieces of fiction, other poetry, and, naturally, scenes from dramatic plays. You might, for example, have students offer different interpretations of the same poem, such as "My Papa's Waltz" by Theodore Roethke. Or, they could take turns reciting narrative ballads such as "The Highwayman" by Alfred Noyes or "Annabelle Lee" by Edgar Allen Poe.

Reflections: *This is a particularly effective activity if your goal is to include more cooperative learning in your classroom. You can vary the amount of student choice that's incorporated into the activity. For example, groups can either be student-selected or teacher-designed. You can assign* *particular groups specific poems, they can choose a poem from a group that you have preselected, or selecting an appropriate poem can be part of the assignment. One caveat to that last suggestion: it's useful to have some kind of connection between all of the poems, whether it's thematic as in the activity outlined above or poems written by the same poet.*

Modifying the Text

The purpose of Scaffolded Reading activities is to ensure that students have success in reading—that they are able to engage in extracting and constructing meaning as they read and will gain new knowledge, new insights, and a sense of accomplishment from their reading. For some students, achieving success requires your presenting a selection in a form that varies from the original. Sometimes because of what is either required by your school district or what is available, the material may simply be too challenging or too lengthy for some students. Unfortunately, this is frequently the case with your less-skilled readers; and with the new Common Core Standards Initiative, it may become even more frequent (for example, see Adams 2010–11). When a selection is too difficult for some of your students and you cannot find a substitute that meets your needs, modifying or shortening the text is a viable option. In both the short run and the long run, students will become much better readers if they read texts they can be successful with.

For some students, achieving success requires your presenting a selection in a form that varies from the original.

There are several ways in which you can modify a text. One is to actually rewrite some or all of it. Although rewriting a text isn't impossible and might be useful sometimes, it is not an option you are likely to use frequently because it's so time consuming. Another way to modify a text is to record it, or parts of it, so that some students can listen to it rather than read it, or perhaps follow along in their text as they listen to it. And it does not have to be you who does the recording. Your more able readers can certainly do some recording. Also, in some cases you may be able to purchase, check out, or download a professional recording of some of the selections your students are reading.

Still another type of modification, and the one we think you are likely to use the most frequently, is to simply have students read only part of a selection. Sometimes it just isn't feasible or even advisable for students to read an entire selection. When lack of time or other constraints make reading an entire selection unadvisable, shortening the reading assignment—for some or all of your students—is one workable option. Shortening the text is one of the most practical and effective ways of differentiating instruction. In shortening a text, you have students read only selected portions of a work—the topics you feel are most important for them to understand. Will students get as much from reading part of a text as from reading all of it? Of course not. Students will miss some things, but assuming they cannot or will not read all of it, success in reading part of it is certainly preferable to failure in reading all of it.

MODIFYING THE TEXT—Emergency Scissors

In *Emergency Scissors*, you assign part of a selection to those students who are capable of reading only part of it. This activity was given its name by Ellen Lamar Thomas, a colleague we worked with some years ago. There are of course no scissors involved; Ellen simply used a metaphor for cutting out part of the text.

Selection: *The House on Mango Street* by Sandra Cisneros. In this award-winning, coming-of-age novel, Cisneros focuses on the challenges of being a woman in the often patriarchal Hispanic world of the barrio. The only girl in a family of seven children, Cisneros grew up in the Puerto Rican neighborhoods of Chicago and thus brings many rich experiences to her exploration of this theme. The book consists of a series of vignettes, some longer and some shorter, and thus is an excellent text for students to sample.

Students: Ninth and tenth graders of varied reading abilities including some English language learners.

Reading Purposes: To understand the novel and its central theme and to consider some of the situations Cisneros' characters face and their relevance to your students' lives and values.

Goals of Activity: To enable all students in a class—good readers and poor readers, native English speakers and English language learners—to understand the book and its themes and to actively engage in discussing it.

Procedure: Decide which vignettes all students will read and which parts will be summarized and not read by all students. Also decide—if you have a number of Spanish-speaking English learners in your classroom—if would be useful and feasible to have at least some of the summaries in Spanish as well as in English. Once you have made these decisions, either write the summaries yourself or share the writing with some of your stronger readers and writers. This is, we believe, an authentic and, therefore, valuable writing task, and if you have students who can do some of the summarizing it should be a worthwhile experience for them. Once the summaries are completed, identify those students who will read the whole of the book and those who will read parts of it and the summaries. You may, of course, want to let the students themselves decide who will read all of the book and who will rely partly on the summaries. In the discussion that is likely to follow the reading, be sure include both students who have read the whole of the book and those who used the summaries in each group.

Other Selections: *Emergency Scissors* is an obvious approach for books like *The House on Mango Street* that are composed of more or less individual vignettes. However, the approach can be used with virtually any book if in your judgment the book is too long and too challenging for some of your students. Thus, it is appropriate—depending again on your students' reading abilities—for books ranging from *A Death in the Family* and *Heart of Darkness* to *The Perks of Being a Wallflower* and *One Good Punch*.

Reflections. *While* Emergency Scissors *will often prove useful, we need to be careful not to use them too frequently. While reading part of a selection is always preferable to not reading any of it, there is no way that reading part of a selection yields everything that reading all of it does. Constructing SREs and tailoring them to your students is always a challenge. The concept of scaffolding is a very powerful one, but choosing just the right amount of scaffolding for a particular student or group of students is always a challenge and a judgment call. We want to stretch students so that they truly become increasingly competent but not so much that they fail or, worse yet, fail to try.*

A Final Word

As she contemplates what sorts of during-reading activities will benefit her students—what kind of reading experience she wants for her students as they read *Monster*—Lizzie considers the kinds of activities that we have presented in this chapter. She considers her students' needs, interests, and abilities; the material they are reading; and their purposes for reading. She knows, for example, that the content of the material is naturally engaging but that the format might be difficult for her less-skilled readers. As is the case with prereading, the purpose of during-reading activities is to provide a scaffold that will ensure students achieve their reading goals. As is also the case with prereading, as well as with postreading, there is also the matter of your time to consider. There simply is not time for you to create all of the activities you might like to, and thus you must focus on creating those that will best help your students succeed in the reading they do. Lizzie chooses a variety of the activities suggested previously including an oral interpretation activity and a modifying the text activity. She knows that she can't employ every possible activity with every text and looks forward to in creating some new activities for the students' next novel, *The Giver*.

CHAPTER 3

Postreading Activities

At its *best*, reading is an active, constructive process. Until we do something with what we have read, until we internalize the meaning we have gleaned, we are a long way from getting the most we can from a text. Postreading activities encourage students to *do* something with the material they have just read, to think—critically, logically, and creatively—about the information and ideas that emerge from their reading and sometimes to transform their thinking into action. When reading recreationally, we often perceive information with very little effort or thought, and that's fine. But for a lot of reading our students do in school, it's not fine.

At its best, reading is an active, constructive process.

In postreading activities, students recall what they've read and demonstrate understanding, but they also do much more. They apply, analyze, synthesize, evaluate, and elaborate on the information and ideas they've gotten from the text and connect that information and those ideas to their prior knowledge—to other things they've read, to information and ideas they already have, and to the world in which they live. Postreading activities are also opportunities for students to extend ideas, to explore new ways of thinking, doing, and seeing—to invent and create, to ponder *what if?* Like pre- and during-reading categories, postreading activities are options.

Questioning

Questioning activities encourage students to think about and react—either orally or in writing—to the information and ideas in the material they have read. Various types of questions can be used, but at least some of them should require higher-level thinking (Beck and McKeown 1981; Booth Olson, and Land 2007; Duke and Pearson 2002; Smith and Wilhelm 2002). Some questions simply assess whether students remember what they have read. Other questions, however, foster students' ability to understand, apply, analyze, synthesize, evaluate, and think metacognitively.

Questioning activities taps into students' innate curiosity about the world and prompt them to think about and respond to information and ideas on a variety of levels.

In addition to introducing students to various types of questions, you need to give them opportunities to be aware of and respond to various audiences. For whom are they answering the questions? Themselves? You? Other students? Various audiences are appropriate; the thing to avoid is always having students respond to a single audience—you.

Although postreading questioning is sometimes used to assess students' reading comprehension and their ability to think at various levels, it should more often allow and encourage students to delve more deeply into the texts they read. Questioning activities taps into students' innate curiosity about the world and prompt them to think about and respond to information and ideas on a variety of levels. The questioning activity below focuses on reader response, just one of the myriad focuses postreading questioning can have.

QUESTIONING—What Do You Think?

In *What Do You Think?* students write personal responses to a question based on a story's main theme. Their responses are then displayed on a reader response chart and shared with the class.

Selection: *Journey*, by Patricia MacLachlan, a compact and well-crafted novel about a boy named Journey whose anger and grief over his mother's abandonment is eventually replaced by acceptance and trust.

Students: Sixth and seventh graders of low to average reading ability.

Reading Purposes: To enjoy a sensitive, well-crafted story and make connections between the ideas developed in the story and one's own life.

Goals of the Activity: To help students feel secure in their response, not depend on someone else's response, and respect other responses.

Procedure:

- Create a large chart with space for each student's picture (ask students to provide one) and her or his written response.

- When they finish the novel, ask them what they think are some important artifacts in the story—items that are especially important to Journey. Cameras and photos are likely to be high on the list. Ask students how cameras and photos were used in the story and why they think these are significant items.

- Now show students the chart and have them paste their picture on one of the spaces. Discuss how their photos reveal their uniqueness. Explain that just as they each have a unique hairstyle, smile, pose, outfit, skin color, and the like, their responses to a piece of literature will also be unique.

- Explain further that each person's picture also reveals the similarities he or she shares with others. Have students point out similarities in their pictures, and note that their responses to this and other novels will also have similarities.

- Explain that as they read more stories and poems it will be fun to see just what the similarities and differences in their responses are.

- Ask students to write a response to the question, "How do you think photographs helped Journey?" (Give them a little time to think about it first or have them start right in.) After students have written their responses, have them post them on the reader response chart next to their photo.

■ Ask each student to read his or her response aloud, and then, as a class, discuss similarities and differences in the responses.

Other Selections: Because photographs are central to the theme of this novel, *Journey* is an ideal springboard for introducing a reader response chart that includes student photos. However, a reader response chart can be used with any work—informational texts like Malcolm Gladwell's *Blink*, traditional novels like John Hersey's *A Bell for Adano*, graphic novels like Sam Kieth's *Zero Girl*.

Reflections: *Sharing personal responses helps students understand the importance and significance of the schema each individual brings to reading—how the meaning one person constructs from a text might be somewhat different from the meaning another person constructs. Students will see that there are common responses as well. However, when constructing personal response questions, be careful not to invade students' privacy. "How did you feel when . . ." questions might be appropriate if students are writing responses in personal journals; they may not be appropriate when there is an audience.*

Discussion

Almost every classroom reading experience will include some sort of discussion— exchanging ideas out loud. The key word is *exchanging*. The intent of discussion is to explore ideas freely, to learn something new or gain a different perspective from a number of people's ideas or insights. Discussion is an active exchange, ideally one in which everyone has the opportunity to participate equally; it is an opportunity to solidify, clarify, or modify knowledge. Discussion activities are a forum in which students talk about the meaning they constructed, listen to the insights of others, and weigh their responses in light of those of their classmates. Students can think about, ponder, consider, analyze, and evaluate. They can make connections between the text and their own lives, as well as among the text, their personal experiences, and the thoughts and experiences of other students.

Discussion groups can be teacher- or student-led. They can involve the entire class, small groups, or pairs. The following discussion activity gives students an opportunity to work in small groups and seek consensus on a topic, although consensus may not be possible.

DISCUSSION—Three's a Charm

In *Three's a Charm*, three groups of students find specific examples of three important concepts in a text and report their findings to the class.

Selection: *Eyes on the Prize: America's Civil Rights Years, 1954–1965*, by Juan Williams. This text, based on an award-winning PBS television series, brings the events of the nonviolent civil rights years to life with lucid writing, gripping photographs, and quotes from participants.

Students: High school students of middle to high reading ability.

Reading Purpose: To understand and appreciate some of the purposes, participants, and methods of the civil rights movement.

Goals of the Activity: To stimulate students' use of recall and critical-thinking skills and to provide an opportunity for students to work together toward a consensus.

Procedure:

- Tell students that the civil rights movement employed a number of different strategies to achieve equal rights but that three were probably used most often and most effectively. Explain that they will get the chance to talk about which three they think were most effective, listen to what others think, and attempt to come to a common agreement.

- Divide the class into three groups and appoint a leader and three recorders for each. Explain that the groups are to meet and decide what they think were the three main tools of the civil rights movement. Instruct students to bring their copy of *Eyes on the Prize* to the group meeting.

- Have each group review the book, identify the three methods, and be ready to give specific examples of each from the text. Students in each group should take turns telling about a strategy and locating examples in the text. After groups decide which they think the three most effective strategies were, each recorder writes down a specific example of one of the strategies.

- Give the groups twenty minutes or so for discussion while you circulate, giving help, encouragement, and praise.

- After the discussions are completed, let the three recorders for each group report their group's findings.

- Compare and contrast each group's answers. Was there a consistency among the three choices? If so, what was the reason for this consistency? Was there discrepancy? If so, can group members defend their choices?

Other Selections: This activity can be used with almost any reading selection; you just have to choose an appropriate question. For example, after reading Martha Brooks' *Confessions of a Heartless Girl*, the question might be, "What do you think is the most important event in the life of each of the three protagonists—Noreen, Lynda, and Dolores—that led them to the situation they were in at the end of the book?" After reading Caroline Alexander's *The Endurance: Shackleton's Legendary Antarctic Expedition*, the prompt could be, "What were the three most important things that helped the twenty-seven men in the Shackleton expedition survive their almost two-year ordeal in the Antarctic?" Also, even though three is the magic number in this example, this activity works with other numbers of items as well, anything from two to six.

Reflections: *Ideally, give students the focusing question before they read so they can be looking for the three big or most important ideas, perhaps using sticky notes or jotting down possibilities in their journal. As this activity so clearly illustrates, pre-, while-, and postreading activities are linked. Students' attention is focused before they read. While they read, they are looking for the big ideas as they construct meaning. After they read, they check their responses against those of others; they evaluate and make decisions based on their ideas, the text, and their group members' ideas. The discussion that follows is always lively as well as illuminating because students tend to have strong ideas about what they perceive as most important.*

Writing

E. M. Forster once wrote, "How can I tell what I think till I see what I say?" (Forester 1956). Writing is the twin sister of reading—a powerful way to integrate what you know with the information presented in a text, as well as to find out what you really understand and what you don't. Writing is powerful because it requires a reader to actively manipulate information and ideas.

Writing is the twin sister of reading.

Obviously, writing is not exclusively a postreading activity. Writing has its place as both a prereading activity—a tool for motivating, activating background knowledge, relating a selection to students' lives—and as a during-reading activity—a device for guiding students' thought processes as they build meaning. As a postreading activity, writing can serve all the purposes listed at the beginning of the chapter—demonstrating understanding of the information and ideas presented in a text; applying, analyzing, synthesizing, evaluating, and elaborating on text information and ideas; and connecting information and ideas in a logical way. Writing also gives students the opportunity to extend ideas, to explore new ways of thinking, doing, seeing—to invent, evaluate, create, and ponder.

With writing activities, two issues go hand in hand—purpose and audience. Why are we encouraging students to write—what purpose does the writing serve? And for whom is the student writing—himself or herself or someone else?

Dividing the purposes of writing into two broad categories—writing to learn and writing to communicate with others—helps you identify the kinds of writing you might encourage students to do after they read a selection, as well as determine the appropriate audience for their writing. However, remember that whether students are writing to learn, to explore, or to communicate, they are actively manipulating ideas and language. The writing activity described here illustrates just one of the many types of writing that can be fruitfully incorporated into reading experiences.

WRITING—A Birthday to Remember

A *Birthday to Remember* uses a short story as a jumping-off point for autobiographical writing. Students are invited to think about memorable incidents from their childhood. The students develop their pieces in cooperative groups and then share them with the class.

Selection: "Eleven," by Sandra Cisneros, from her collection *Woman Hollering Creek*. Reminiscent of the voice used in *The House on Mango Street*, the story is written in the first person, as an eleven-year-old recounts an embarrassing incident on her birthday.

Students: Middle school students, grades 6–8. (The activity can also be adapted for high school students.)

Reading Purposes: To become familiar with the voice and style of Sandra Cisneros and to make connections to autobiographical incidents that relate to the text.

Goals of the Activity: To extend students' engagement with the text through an autobiographical writing exercise and to give students more experience with narrative writing

Procedure:

- After reading "Eleven," discuss the following questions: *What is particularly important to children about their birthday? How was this birthday ruined? Is there any chance the birthday can be saved?*
- Give students a timeline and ask them to fill in one memorable aspect of each birthday they have celebrated.
- Have students, in small groups, help one another choose which birthday event to write about using the following criteria:
  - ▶ Can you remember enough detail?
  - ▶ Is it worth remembering?
  - ▶ Will it be interesting to other people?
  - ▶ Is there a larger point to the story?

- ■ Ask students to write a two- or three-page birthday memory, using a style similar to that of Cisneros: short sentences and simple words in a childlike voice. (They can finish and polish up their pieces at home.)
- ■ The next day have students read their pieces aloud and discuss them as a class:
  - ▸ What themes are common to all the pieces?
  - ▸ In what ways are they similar to "Eleven"?
  - ▸ In what ways are they different from "Eleven"?

Other Selections: This activity can be used with many selections, especially memoir or autobiographically based fiction. Isolate critical incidents in the text and have students extend their understanding and comprehension by writing about them. (Extend the activity by inviting students to write about a series of memories.)

Reflections: *Writing on a similar theme in a similar style helps students connect the act of writing with the text they have read. Although it might be possible to use a version of this example as a prereading activity, doing so spoils the surprise that it is the narrator's birthday; therefore, it's more effective as a postreading exercise.*

Drama

Drama is a natural part of childhood. As soon as their language and social skills begin to develop, children play "house," "doctor," and "school." They enact dramas with their dolls, trucks, cars, or representations of their favorite cartoon, movie, and TV characters. Children not only participate in these playtime dramas but also create them. Through drama, children translate what they know about the world into dialogue and body language. This natural interest in drama extends through adolescence. Postreading drama activities encourage students to extend existing meanings and generate new ones. And they're fun, highly motivating ways to involve students in all the cognitive tasks we listed at the beginning of the chapter—applying, analyzing, synthesizing, and evaluating.

Through drama, children translate what they know about the world into dialogue and body language.

In postreading dramatic activities, students combine the meaning they have constructed from the text, the resources available to them, and their own ideas to produce a "play" with settings, characters, dialogue, action, and props. It might be a one-minute pantomime involving just one actor or a fifty-minute production starring everyone in the class and featuring props, costumes, and lighting.

Dramatic activities can be used with fiction, nonfiction, or poetry. Dramatizing requires all sorts of decisions. What will I say? How will I say it? What actions and facial expressions will I use? What costumes or props will I need? Will I need to play more than one part?

Although an audience is sometimes appropriate, dramatizations don't require one. The audience can consist of only the students enacting the drama. After reading a chapter about the sixties in a history or social studies text, for example, two seventh or eighth graders might decide to portray Martin Luther King, Jr., and Lyndon B. Johnson. First they need to gather information about these men—policies, actions, attitudes, style of speech. Then they need to select a topic—what would Martin Luther King, Jr., and Lyndon B. Johnson talk to each other about? For the dramatization, students carry on a conversation posing as these individuals. The dramatization could end here, or students might choose to perform it for other students or for an even larger audience such as another class or parents. Although they don't need to be performed for other audiences, these dramas could be performed in places such as day care centers or nursing homes.

You'll need to play a variety of roles, depending on the students, the selection, and the purpose of the activity. Occasionally, you might become the director/producer, but more often your job will be that of facilitator/encourager. You might play the role of the narrator in *Our Town,* read stage directions from a Shakespeare play, or moderate solutions and compromises when problems arise.

Drama has great potential for showing students that written language can be transformed into oral language and that ideas can be seen, heard, and felt, as this sample activity demonstrates.

DRAMA—You Are There

In *You Are There*, students extend their knowledge of characters beyond the text by acting out several hypothetical scenarios in which the characters might find themselves.

Selection: *Of Mice and Men.* The strong characters and simple language in this short, widely taught novel are very appealing and accessible.

Students: Eighth to tenth graders of mixed abilities.

Reading Purpose: To become familiar with a classic text and gain a solid understanding of how character drives plot.

Goal of the Activity: To help students solidify their understanding of the characters through creative dramatics.

Procedure:

- Divide students into small groups and assign each group a main character: George, Lenny, Curly, Curly's wife, Crooks, and Candy. Tell the students to become experts in their assigned character by noting relevant quotations, descriptions, and major incidents from the novel.

- Pass out several scenarios:

  ▶ George and Candy find some money that was dropped in one of the horse stalls. Will they try to find out who lost the money, or will they keep it for themselves?

  ▶ Crooks and Candy are bullied at a dinner that everyone attends. They are teased relentlessly about the fact that Crooks is black and Candy is old and crippled. Who will come to their rescue?

  ▶ George is put on trial for Lenny's murder and the rest of the characters are called to the stand to defend him. What will they say?

  ▶ What are the characters' lives like ten years after the novel ends? Where are they now?

- Have a student from each group, using what he or she knows about the character, participate in a three- to five-minute sketch based on one of these scenarios.

- After each improvisation, have the whole class discuss whether the improvisation was consistent with the characters as they are presented in the novel.

Additional Selections: This activity can be used with a wide variety of novels and short stories. Character-driven stories such as *To Kill a Mockingbird, Peace Like a River, The Secret Lives of Bees, The Great Gatsby*, and *Beloved* are all excellent choices.

Reflections: *Students of all grade levels enjoy this unique way to read and respond to literary texts. Of Mice and Men has been an enduring entry in the secondary school literature canon for decades. There is little chance that it will cease to be taught in favor of more contemporary selections, nor are we arguing that it should be replaced. However, like all canonical works, it runs the risk of being taught as a static set piece. By having the characters come alive in a dramatic role-play, you breathe life into the novel by breathing life into its characters.*

Artistic, Graphic, and Nonverbal Activities

This category includes the visual arts, music, and dance—each a specialized language that can be used to respond to printed and spoken communication. It also includes audiotapes, videos, slideshows; visual displays such as bulletin boards, artifacts, and specimens; and visual representations of information such as graphs, maps, and charts. Each of these varied forms of expression is a special way for students to deepen and broaden their understanding of the ideas and information in the texts they read. Each also gives students who may struggle with verbal skills and English learners whose English is not fully developed a way to express themselves that doesn't require verbal dexterity.

In the following sample activity, based on an SRE created by Eric Zuccola, a teacher at Robbinsdale Cooper High School in Minnesota, we give an example of senior high students working on a project that provides the opportunity for both verbal and nonverbal expression.

ARTISTIC, GRAPHIC, AND NONVERBAL—Art Project

Art Project gives students an opportunity to select a significant event or sequence of events from a contemporary text and represent that event or sequence in both verbal and nonverbal ways.

Selection: *Night Flying Woman*, by Ignatia Broker. In this accessible and gripping novel, Broker recounts the life of her great-great-grandmother, Night Flying Woman, an Ojibway who lived in Minnesota during the mid-nineteenth century.

Students: High school students—some of whom are English learners—with markedly varied levels of proficiency in English.

Reading Purposes: To understand the rich characters, themes, images, and events depicted in *Night Flying Woman* and to appreciate the craft Ignatia Broker employs in presenting these characters, themes, and events.

Goals of the Activity: To use both nonverbal and verbal skills to create an artistic display capturing an event or sequence of events from this rich narrative and to share this display with the class.

Procedure:

- Have students work on this project individually or in pairs (perhaps pair an English learner with a native English speaker).
- Give them the following assignment:
  ▸ Creatively, accurately, and appropriately, using drawings, graphics, pictures, a collage, or some combination thereof, make a poster depicting a significant event or sequence of events from *Night Flying Woman*.
  ▸ Include in your display a direct quote from the text relevant to the event or sequence you are depicting.
  ▸ Write, edit, and proof a 100-word explanation of why the event or sequence you are depicting is significant to the text. Hang this from the bottom of your poster.
  ▸ Your work will be judged on originality, accuracy, clarity of purpose, the significance of the event, and artistic merit.

- Let them work on their poster for about twenty minutes a day over three days. (They will also gather material outside class.)
- Have them hand in their work on the third day.
- Hang the posters that night so they can view the "art show" when they come to class the next day.

Other Selections: This project can be used with any text dealing with meaningful themes and including notable events and sequences of events (which is a lot of texts!). For example: Michael Blake's *Dances with Wolves,* which deals with some of the same themes and settings as *Night Flying Woman*; Stephen Crane's *The Red Badge of Courage,* with its vivid Civil War images; or something more contemporary, like Chuck Palahniuk's *Fight Club.*

Reflections: *Because of the opportunities an activity like this gives to students who are still developing their English skills, it is particularly appropriate for English learners. However, we do not mean to suggest that artistic, graphic, and nonverbal activities are appropriate only for English learners. All students need to have opportunities to express themselves and respond to what they read in a variety of ways.*

Application and Outreach

Books open doors. They invite us to step out, go beyond the text to see for ourselves, act on our newfound knowledge, apply it in a unique way. All the previously mentioned categories in one way or another help students go beyond the text to explore other realms and other applications of information and ideas.

In endeavors specifically labeled as application and outreach, students take the ideas and information from a text and deliberately test, use, or explore it. They might read an article on how to make friends, but the information has little value unless students try out the author's ideas to see whether they work. They might read a story about making ice cream or an article describing a science experiment, but it's not as much fun as making ice cream from a recipe and then eating it or replicating the experiments in Sandra Markle's *Science Mini-Mysteries.* A logical next step after reading about something is to try it out in the real world.

It is not only how-to books, however, that invite real-world applications. A chapter on the environment in a science text may inspire students to do something themselves to better care for Earth. After finishing a novel in which the main character has a disability, a reader might change his or her attitude about persons with disabilities and begin to act differently toward them. Application and outreach activities invite and encourage many different kinds of personal and social action.

A logical next step after reading about something is to try it out in the real world.

The fiction, nonfiction, and poetry students read can open doors to the wider world. Students reading the classic "Rikki-Tikki-Tavi" can imagine exotic worlds that exist beyond their immediate geographical boundaries. Nikki Giovanni's poems describe what it feels like to grow up in Chicago, and Tim O' Brien takes adolescent readers to the jungles of Vietnam.

Outreach activities can not only take children beyond the school walls in order to explore a topic or idea further or discover more but also inspire them to social action.

Outreach activities can not only take children beyond the school walls in order to explore a topic or idea further or discover more but also inspire them to social action. However, students will not always make the connections necessary to transfer ideas from the text to the real world on their own. By providing activities that demonstrate this connection, you can drive home a critical aspect of the nature of text—we should not be the same after we have read it. We are a little more than we were before. Our new selves contain new information and ideas that we can now use. The following activity shows one way students might apply what they have discovered in a text by reaching out to others.

APPLICATION AND OUTREACH—Community Gardens

Community Gardens encourages students to participate in a community activity thematically tied to a story about the destruction of an elderly neighbor's garden.

Selection: "Marigolds," by Eugenia Collier, a story about a young girl who commits a senseless act of vandalism against an elderly neighbor. The story has a classic narrative structure and well-drawn characters and is widely available in short story collections and literature textbooks.

Students: Tenth and eleventh graders of mixed ability.

Reading Purposes: To better understand the short story genre and its ability to portray strong themes and characters efficiently in a relatively condensed narrative space and to think about bullying (increasingly present in contemporary schools) and intergenerational conflict.

Goals of the Activity: Extend the themes of the story into the students' lived experiences; give students an opportunity to engage in community service.

Procedure:

- Have students read the story.
- Discuss the importance of the marigolds to Miss Lottie and why the main character Lizbeth is compelled to destroy them.
- Take students on two visits to a senior residential center:

> ▸ On the first visit, have students interview residents about their favorite plants and flowers and then compile a list of these flowers and plants to purchase from a local nursery.

> ▸ On the second visit, have students plant the flowers and plants they have purchased and place a plaque next to each one bearing the name of the senior resident in whose honor it is planted.

■ Ask students to write a journal entry reflecting on their experience and connecting the people they met with Miss Lottie of the story.

Other Selections: Barbara Huff's *Greening the City Streets: The Story of Community Gardens* might inspire urban seventh graders to plan and develop community gardens in their neighborhood. After reading *To Kill a Mockingbird* or *The Watsons Go to Birmingham—1963*, students might participate in the continuing struggle for racial equality by contacting their legislators about relevant local issues; equally important, they might identify ways in which our daily lives are marked by subtle and not so subtle examples of racial inequity.

Reflections: *School-based civic involvement is an increasingly important way to make learning meaningful and relevant to our students' lives outside school. Like Mayella's geraniums in* To Kill a Mockingbird, *the marigolds in this story are a critical oasis of beauty in an otherwise desolate Depression-era existence. Civic involvement also provides a context in which to consider contemporary concerns about bullying and groupthink.*

Building Connections

Since application and outreach activities offer students many opportunities to build connections, why include a separate section on building connections activities? Well, a great deal of educational theory over the past thirty years—from David Rumelhart's early work on schema (1980) to more contemporary reports such those of the RAND Reading Study Group (Snow 2001) and the National Institute for Literacy (2007), to the current interest in a common core curriculum (*American Educator* 2010–11)—highlights the huge importance of children's store of organized knowledge to their learning and success in and out of school. Building connections—establishing links among the vast array of schemas that students internalize—is important whether students are reading narratives or exposition; factual material or fiction; history, science, English, or any other subject.

We want children to build connections in several directions:

1. We want students to realize that what they bring to school—the wealth of real-world experiences that they bring with them when they enter

kindergarten or first grade and that are constantly enriched each year—is relevant to their being able to understand and make sense of what they are learning in school. (For example, the pride they felt when they were first allowed to go to the grocery store alone helps them empathize with a story character's feelings when she successfully meets some challenge, and they may be able to express that empathy in their writing.)

2. We want students to realize that the various subjects they deal with in school are interrelated in many ways. (For example, the understanding of the Revolutionary War period they gain in social studies can help them understand some of the motives of Johnny in Esther Forbes' *Johnny Tremain*.)

3. We want students to realize that ideas and concepts learned in school are relevant to their lives outside school. (For example, a story character's finding that persistence pays off in meeting her goal suggests that similar persistence may pay off in getting a younger brother to quit leaving his toys scattered all over a shared bedroom.)

Very little that we do as teachers is more important than helping students build these sorts of connections. The following activity provides one example of how we can do so.

BUILDING CONNECTIONS—What They Still Carry

What They Still Carry encourages students to build connections to the text by considering contemporary wars and thinking about individual troops and their possessions.

Selection: "The Things They Carried," the opening story of the acclaimed Tim O'Brien novel of the same name. The stories can be taught individually or as a whole unit. The text ties in perfectly with a consideration of genre, since it is both fiction and autobiography.

Students: Tenth, eleventh, and twelfth graders of mixed abilities.

Reading Purpose: To experience how modern fiction uses real events as a basis for creating literary art.

Goals of the Activity: To help students see that the themes and portraits of war that are so evocatively portrayed in O'Brien's book unfortunately still exist today and to make interdisciplinary connections between students' study of history and current events and their literary experiences.

Procedures:

- ■ Have students read "The Things They Carried."
- ■ Have them list all the objects that were carried in the soldiers' backpacks.
- ■ Have them read two contemporary articles and watch several newscasts on the theaters of war in Afghanistan and Iraq.
- ■ Have students, in groups of three, list what a contemporary soldier might carry in his or her backpack. In keeping with the themes and focus of O'Brien's story, this list should include personal items as well as items that might be standard issue.
- ■ Ask each group to share their list.
- ■ Have students write a page-long reflection on what themes from the story are represented in their artifacts, what aspects of war seem to have changed since the Vietnam era, and what aspects seem to have remained essentially constant.

Other Selections: The activity could also be used as a postreading activity for the entire book *The Things They Carried* or adapted to other war-themed novels, including *The Red Badge of Courage, All Quiet on the Western Front, Cold Mountain,* and *A Farewell to Arms.* It could be used in conjunction with critical viewings of classic and contemporary films about war, including *Saving Private Ryan, The Hurt Locker, Flags of Our Fathers, The Deer Hunter,* and *Platoon.*

Reflections: *The Things They Carried is a very teachable book. O'Brien conveys his perspective by materializing the effects of war, making them concrete. Although decades have passed since the end of the Vietnam War, O'Brien's prose raises timeless issues. In addition, the book seems to engage even the most reluctant readers. You can read excerpts or the whole book. We enthusiastically suggest the latter.*

Reteaching

Like many other types of SRE activities, reteaching can and should take place whenever it becomes apparent that it is necessary. If you introduce a selection and look up to a sea of blank faces, or if students are reading silently and you recognize signs of confusion or frustration, you have an opening for reteaching. A focus of reteaching will often be to encourage students to self-evaluate, to become metacognitive readers. After all, while you are there to encourage and assist, it is the student who is ultimately responsible for his or her own learning. In the following Reteaching activity, however, the teacher does a lot of work after realizing that the initial assignment was just too difficult.

RETEACHING—Play It Again, Sam

In *Play It Again, Sam*, a previous lesson is restructured and strengthened as an aid to students who did not succeed in their initial attempts with a selection. In this case, we are assuming that students were given a traditional study activity asking them to summarize some stories in Chaucer's *Canterbury Tales* and that it became apparent as they were working on their summaries that the class as a whole needed more help.

Selection: *The Canterbury Tales*, by Geoffrey Chaucer.

Students: Eleventh and twelfth graders of mixed abilities.

Reading Purpose: To familiarize students with some of Chaucer's better-known tales.

Goal of the Original Activity: By having each of half a dozen or so groups read one of the tales and then present a summary of their tales to the class, all students were expected to gain some knowledge of Chaucer's work without the class as a whole spending the time that reading all 300-plus pages of the manuscript would require.

Goal of the Supplementary Activity: As we said, students were floundering at the summarizing task, hence this reteaching activity. As we said in Chapter 2 when we described the original activity, traditional study activities generally ask students to do something without providing them with much support. As was obvious from the students floundering, our original activity did not provide them with enough support. This time we will more fully explain and model how to write the summaries.

Procedure:

- Share your recognition that students are having difficulty summarizing the stories; acknowledge that you did not provide enough guidance; and tell them you will now explain summarizing more fully, create a model summary, and ask them to summarize only a part of their tales.

- Announce that scholars have developed some general rules for summarizing and that you have attempted to follow these rules in preparing your model summary. The rules (slightly modified from Brown and Day 1983), are:

  1. **Delete trivial or irrelevant information.**
  2. **Delete redundant information.**
  3. **Provide a superordinate term for members of a category.**
  4. **Find and use generalizations the author has made.**
  5. **Create your own generalizations when the author has not provided them.**

- Admit to students that even with these rules to guide them, when they summarize complex material like *The Canterbury Tales*, they will have to rely heavily on intuition and discard a lot of information.

- Note that because of the amount of detail in *The Canterbury Tales*, they will be summarizing only the first 50–100 lines of their tale.
- Summarize "The Monk's Tale" as an example.
- Have students read a modern version of the introduction and the stories of Lucifer and Adam (about fifty lines).
- When they finish, read aloud and summarize each section in turn.
  - For the introductory paragraph, your summary might be: "The stories I am going to tell you are tragedies, and tell of how people of high status fell from prosperity and into ruin."
  - For the story of Lucifer, your summary might be: "Lucifer, the brightest of all angels and of higher status than any human, sinned and fell into hell, where he remains."
  - For the story of Adam, your summary might be: "Adam ruled all of Paradise except one tree and had the highest status of any man. But Adam committed a misdeed and was driven to Hell."
- Have groups return to the tale they are to summarize, noting again that they need summarize only the first 50–100 lines, and circulate among the groups offering further scaffolding if necessary.

Other Selections: Reteaching may prove necessary with any selection, although you will need to do so more frequently with more difficult tests.

Reflections: *Obviously, the initial instruction here was not successful. But the need to reteach doesn't signify failure. You fail only if you give students a task they cannot complete and ignore their lack of success. A major premise underlying SREs is that when you present students with challenging tasks, you need to provide them with the scaffolding to complete those tasks successfully. Much of learning comes from attempting and completing challenging tasks. When the scaffolding we originally provide is insufficient—and it will almost certainly be insufficient from time to time—we simply need to provide more support.*

A Final Word

Many of the postreading activities described in this section are traditionally thought of as "enrichment" activities. And indeed they are, for they do enrich the reader. But we need to be careful when we use this label that we are being *in*clusive and not *ex*clusive in selecting students who will be enriched. If we think of *all* students who read as *rich*—those who flounder as well as those who soar—then we need to be certain to provide activities that will enrich them all. Sometimes, students who struggle with the basics, who lack traditional literacy skills, have been left out of these activities and thus have not been allowed the

If we think of all students who read as rich—those who flounder as well as those who soar— then we need to be certain to provide activities that will enrich them all.

opportunities for the growth that enrichment activities can provide. All students deserve and will benefit from a variety of postreading activities and should be given opportunities to explore as many of them as possible.

Activities that students engage in after reading drive home the fact that reading has purpose—they can actually *do* something with the ideas in books. They can make connections between what they know and what they discover in texts and apply that new knowledge so that their lives become more enjoyable, more productive, and more meaningful.

CHAPTER 4

Lenses for Approaching Literary Texts

Literary theory—critical frames or perspectives for reading texts, such as reader response, formalist, gender, postcolonial, psychoanalytic—is no longer the exclusive province of college classrooms but has found its way into secondary classrooms as well. Considering contemporary literary theory helps us introduce the concept of multiple perspectives to our students. Multiple perspectives help students see a text from several points of view and give them a variety of ways to enter a text. This multiplicity is especially important in our increasingly diverse classrooms.

Literary theory is also heralded as a tool to engage reluctant readers (Eckert 2006) and a pedagogical frame for teaching young adult literature (Soter, Faust, and Rogers 2008). Recently, a major literature anthology for grades 6–12 used literary theory as one of its organizing principles, thus acknowledging its status as a mainstream pedagogy.

One of the common misconceptions about literary theory in secondary classrooms is that it should be used primarily with advanced students in the upper grades. Nothing could be further from the truth. Literary theory can be successfully used as a classroom strategy with a wide variety of students, beginning as early as grade 6. We should, of course, vary the complexity of the lenses used (as well as the texts), but that is simply good teaching.

Literary theory can be successfully used as a classroom strategy with a wide variety of students, beginning as early as grade 6.

Getting Started: Prereading Activities

One way to begin is to emphasize the idea of multiple perspectives or multiple ways of *seeing* rather than introduce the heady and sometimes overly academic concept of literary theory.

A good book to use for this purpose is *The True Story of the Three Little Pigs by A. Wolf*, by Jon Scieszka (1989), in which the familiar childhood story is told from the wolf's perspective. (A sample lesson is provided below.) This perspective naturally changes everything: the wolf was innocent, he was framed, and the pigs were manipulative and greedy. The teller of the tale changes the tale.

Once this notion of perspective is introduced, extend students' understanding by asking them to consider family stories and how each family member may have a different perspective on the same event.

A MATTER OF PERSPECTIVE

Introduction: "Most postmodern fiction violates traditional narrative expectations by telling the story from the perspective of a variety of characters, rather than from the perspective of a single protagonist. Let's spend this period exploring the notion of perspective."

Procedure:

- "Someone tell us the story of the three little pigs."
- "Now I'm going to read you the children's book *The True Story of the Three Little Pigs by A. Wolf*."
- "What differences does that switch in perspective make?"
- "Think of a family story, preferably one that is retold often, a part of your family mythology. In a paragraph or so, tell that story from your own perspective."
- "Now think of another family member, and retell the story from his/her perspective. In groups of no more than four, share those stories and discuss the difference perspective makes. How can we know what is the 'true' version of the story?"

You can also stage an unusual event—a clown (or an animal) invading the classroom, an argument between two class members, a visit from the principal or a fellow teacher wearing a strange costume—then ask students to write down exactly what happened. Compare their versions, discuss the inevitable discrepancies, and call attention to the documented fallibility of eyewitnesses. Next, talk about the kinds of things—beliefs, attitudes, prior experiences, predispositions—that affect both our perceptions of contemporary events as well as our reading.

Introducing Literary Lenses

Students are now ready to be introduced to particular literary theories. Although you may feel uncomfortable teaching literary theory, remember that you're not writing a textbook on the subject, you're just presenting a basic outline. There are many short descriptions available (see Appleman 2000; Beach, Appleman, Hynds, and Wilhelm 2006). Deborah's glossary titled "Literary Perspectives Toolkit" (Appleman 2009) is particularly useful. You might first apply these lenses to films that lend themselves to a spectrum of readings from archetypal to poststructural: *Star Wars*, any episode of *The Lord of the Rings* trilogy, or *Shrek*.

LITERARY PERSPECTIVES TOOLKIT

"If all you have is a hammer, everything looks like a nail."
—Mark Twain

Literary perspectives help us explain why people might interpret the same text in a variety of ways. Perspectives help us understand what is important to individual readers, and they show us why those readers end up seeing what they see. One way to imagine a literary perspective is to think of it as a lens through which we can examine a text. No single lens gives us the clearest view, but it is sometimes fun to read a text with a particular perspective in mind, because we often end up seeing something intriguing and unexpected. While readers typically apply more than one perspective at a time, the best way to understand these perspectives is to use them one at a time. The following descriptions of some of the best-known literary perspectives are extremely brief and don't explain everything, but they should give you a solid understanding about how to use them.

Reader Response. This perspective focuses on the activity of reading. Reader response critics turn away from the traditional idea that a literary work is an artifact with built-in meaning; they attend instead to the responses of individual readers. With this shift of perspective, a literary work is converted into an activity in

---

(continues)

(continued)

the reader's mind. The features of the work itself—including narrator, plot, characters, style, and structure—are less important than the interplay between the reader's experience and the text. Advocates of this perspective believe that literature has no inherent or intrinsic meaning waiting to be discovered. Instead, readers construct meaning as they bring their own thoughts, moods, and experiences to whatever text they are reading. In turn, what readers get out of a text depends on their own expectations and ideas. For example, if you read "Sonny's Blues," by James Baldwin, and you have your own troubled younger brother or sister, the story will have meaning for you that it would not have for an only child.

Archetypal. In literary criticism, an *archetype* is a recognizable pattern or model. The term is used to describe story structure, character types, or images in a wide variety of works. It can also be applied to myths, dreams, and social rituals. The archetypal similarities among texts and behavior are thought to reflect a set of universal, even primitive ways of seeing the world. When found in literary works, they evoke strong responses. Archetypal themes include the heroic journey and the search for a father figure. Archetypal images include the opposition of Paradise and Hades, the river as a sign of life and movement, and mountains or other high places as sources of enlightenment. Characters can be archetypal as well, like the rebel-hero, the scapegoat, the villain, and the goddess.

Formalist. The word *formal* has two related meanings, and both apply within this perspective. The first relates to its root word, *form*, a shape or structure that we can recognize and use to make associations. The second relates to a set of conventions or accepted practices. Formal poetry, for example, has meter, rhyme, stanza, and other predictable features that it shares with poems of the same type. The formalist perspective pays particular attention to these issues of form and convention. Instead of looking at the world in which a poem exists, for example, the formalist perspective says that a poem should be treated as an independent and self-sufficient object. The methods used in this perspective are those of close reading: a detailed and subtle analysis of the formal components that make up the literary work, such as the meanings and interactions of words, figures of speech, and symbols.

Character. Some literary critics call this the "psychological" perspective because it examines the internal motivations of literary characters. Actors who say they are searching for their character's motivation are using something akin to this perspective. As a form of criticism, this perspective deals with works of literature as expressions of the personality, state of mind, feelings, and desires of the author or of a character in the story. As readers, we investigate the psychology of a character or an author to figure out the meaning of a text. (An examination of the author's psychology is sometimes considered biographical criticism, see below.)

Biographical. Because authors typically write about things they care deeply about and know well, the events and circumstances of their lives are often reflected in the literary works they create. For this reason, some readers use biographical information about an author to gain insight into that author's works. This lens, called *biographical criticism*, can be both helpful and dangerous. It can provide insight into themes, historical references, social upheavals or movements, and the creation of fictional characters. At the same time, it is not safe to assume that biographical details from the author's life can be transferred to a story or character the author has created. For example, Ernest Hemingway and John Dos Passos were both ambulance drivers during World War I, and both wrote novels about the war. Their experiences gave them firsthand knowledge and generated strong personal feelings about the war, but their stories are still works of fiction. Some biographical details, in fact, may be completely irrelevant to the interpretation of that writer's work.

Historical. When applying this perspective, you have to view a literary text within its historical context. Specific historical information will be of key interest: the time during which an author wrote, the time in which the text is set, and the ways in which people of the period saw and thought about the world in which they lived. History, in this case, refers to the social, political, economic, cultural, and/or intellectual climate of the time. For example, the literary works of William Faulkner frequently reflect the history of the American South, the Civil War and its aftermath, and the birth and death of a nation known as The Confederate States of America.

Social Power. Some critics believe that human history and institutions, even our ways of thinking, are determined by the ways in which our societies are organized. Two primary factors shape this organization: economic power and social class. First, the class to which we belong determines our degree of economic, political, and social advantage, and the social classes invariably find themselves in conflict with each other. Second, our membership in a social class has a profound impact on our beliefs, values, perceptions, and ways of thinking and feeling. People from different social classes understand the same circumstances in very different ways. When we see members of different social classes thrown together in the same story, we are likely to think in terms of power and advantage as we attempt to explain what happens and why.

Gender. Men and women see things differently. For example, a feminist critic might see cultural and economic disparities as the products of a patriarchal society shaped and dominated by men, who tend to decide things by various means of competition. Because women are frequently brought up to be more cooperative than competitive, they may find that such competition has hindered or prevented them from realizing their full potential, from turning their creative possibilities into action. In addition, societies often tend to see the male perspective as the default, the one we choose automatically. As a result, women are identified as the "other," the deviating or contrasting type. When we use this lens, we examine patterns of thought, behavior, value, and power in relations between the sexes.

Deconstruction. Deconstruction is a difficult critical method to understand at first, because it asks us to set aside ways of thinking that are natural and comfortable. For example, we frequently see the world as a set of opposing categories: male/female, rational/irrational, powerful/powerless. Deconstruction sets aside the ways we assign value to one thing over another, such as life over death, presence over absence, and writing over speech. At its heart, deconstruction is a mode of analysis that asks us to question the very assumptions we bring to that analysis. Gender, for example, is a "construct," a set of beliefs and assumptions that we have built, or constructed, over time and experience. But if we "deconstruct" gender, looking

(continues)

(continued)

at it while holding aside our internalized beliefs and expectations, new understandings become possible. To practice this perspective, then, we must constantly ask ourselves why we believe what we do about the makeup of our world and the ways in which we know it. Then, we must try to explain that world in the absence of our old beliefs.

Scaffolding Reading Experiences and Literary Lenses

Text selection is a key factor in your students' reading success.

Once students have some familiarity with the lenses, you can incorporate them into a Scaffolded Reading Experience. Text selection is a key factor in your students' reading success. If you select texts that are beyond students' current reading abilities or even their zones of proximal development—that is, the reading potential they could reach with appropriate scaffolding—they will be frustrated, and so will you. Conversely, if you select texts that are too simple or unchallenging, students will not be motivated to read. A happy medium, especially in today's increasingly diverse classrooms, is to select texts that are relatively easy to read but can be interpreted on a variety of levels.

The lessons below illustrate how to incorporate literary lenses into Scaffolded Reading Experiences. The texts—"Oranges," by Gary Soto, and the short story "She Unnames Them," by Ursula Le Guin—are accessible to students with a range of reading abilities, yet they hold many interpretive possibilities and can be considered through multiple perspectives.

"ORANGES" SCAFFOLDED READING EXPERIENCE

Materials:

Biography of Gary Soto
Literary Perspectives Toolkit
"Oranges," by Gary Soto
"Oranges": Three Perspectives

Prereading Activities:

- *Building background knowledge*: Review the literary lenses as described in Literary Perspectives Toolkit.

- *Building background knowledge*: Have students read and discuss the biographical sketch of Gary Soto.

- *Relating reading to students' lives*: Assign the following prewriting activity:

  Think about a time when you wanted to give someone something as a way to show how you felt about them. Jot down your memory in six to eight sentences.

Biography of Gary Soto

Gary Soto is an author true to his heritage and culture. He was born in Fresno, California, of Mexican American parents. His education includes a degree in English from California State University at Fresno and a master of arts degree in fine arts and creative writing. He has been a professor at the University of California at Berkeley. He is an acclaimed poet, essayist, and fiction writer.

Soto bases much of his work on his own boyhood experiences. The Central Valley of California is central to the action in many of Soto's books. The streets and neighborhoods of Fresno, California, are an integral part of his writing. He has said, "For me streets have always mattered. I conjure up inside my head an image of our old street in south Fresno." The area where he grew up was much like the barrios he writes about, with junkyards and big factories. In his biographical essays for younger readers ("Living Up the Street," for example) he speaks of playing in Little League and attending parochial school.

Soto also uses some of his own family members as characters in his stories, like "El Shorty" [an uncle], in "Boys at Work." He uses his many memories from childhood to bring life to his short stories and poetry. He tries in his work to regain the losses of childhood and adolescence. Instead of "losing family, deep friends, a place in childhood and finally ourselves," he recalls the blacktop streets he faced, the fruits he would sometimes steal from a neighbor's garden, the bicycle hand brake that became a summer's-day toy for a bored five-year-old. These memories and countless others form the core of his writings. In his collection of poetry, *Neighborhood Odes*, he relives playing in sprinklers and eating snow cones.

Although his stories deal with mostly economically disadvantaged people, they never dwell on the negative but on the problems, solutions, and consequences that many Mexican American families experienced. Soto and other Latino authors have highlighted the culture of a colorful, family-oriented people who know what it means to find work to help the family survive.

(continues)

(continued)

During-Reading Activities:

■ *Silent reading*: Have students read the poem silently.

■ *Guided reading*: Have students read the poem together in pairs, using colored pencils to underline key phrases and mark passages about which they have questions.

■ *Oral reading*: Read the poem aloud as a class, emphasizing the phrases students have marked

Postreading Activities:

■ *Questioning*: Record the key phrases on the board or a transparency and have students summarize them, noting any patterns and repetitions.

■ *Application and outreach*: Divide students into groups of four. Have students complete and discuss the Three Perspectives handout.

■ *Discussion*: Reconvene the whole class and discuss each literary perspective.

■ *Reteaching*: Conclude the lesson by asking students to offer at least three oral interpretations of the poem.

"Oranges": Three Perspectives

Reader Response Perspective

Reread the poem with these questions in mind and then discuss them with three of your classmates:

- What family photos of your own come to mind as you read the poem?
- Who is your usual family photographer? Why?
- What might people be able to tell about your family from the photographs?

Formalist Perspective

Reread the poem with these questions in mind and then discuss them with three of your classmates:

- List some of the images that are conjured up as you read the poem.
- In what ways is this different from most poems you've read?
- How would you describe the tone of the poem? Support your response with specific lines or phrases from the poem.

Biographical Perspective

Read the brief biography of Gary Soto that you were given. Then reread the poem with these questions in mind and discuss them with three of your classmates:

- What images or specific references do the two pieces share?
- What else do the pieces seem to have in common?
- In what ways does the information in the biography affect your reading of the poem?

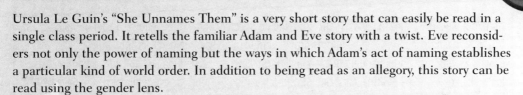

"SHE UNNAMES THEM" SCAFFOLDED READING EXPERIENCE*

Ursula Le Guin's "She Unnames Them" is a very short story that can easily be read in a single class period. It retells the familiar Adam and Eve story with a twist. Eve reconsiders not only the power of naming but the ways in which Adam's act of naming establishes a particular kind of world order. In addition to being read as an allegory, this story can be read using the gender lens.

Materials:

　Literary Perspectives Toolkit
　"She Unnames Them," by Ursula Le Guin
　Literary Theory: Naming What She Unnames

Prereading Activities:

- *Building background knowledge*: Review the literary lenses using the glossary.
- *Activating background knowledge*: Have students retell the Adam and Eve story, first in pairs and then as a whole class.

During-Reading Activities:

- *Silent reading*: Have students read the story individually, circling puzzling words and highlighting important phrases.
- *Guided reading*: Ask each student to compile a list of at least five "I wonder" statements about the text.
- *Oral reading by students/discussion*: Midway through the reading, stop and discuss the "I wonder" statements compiled thus far and discuss each.

(continues)

*Thanks to Kylene Beers for first introducing us to this story.

(continued)

Postreading Activities:

■ *Questioning*: Divide students into groups of three. Assign each group one of these lenses: reader response, feminist, or social hierarchy.

■ *Discussion*: Facilitate as each group discusses their assigned lens and group members answer the questions in the Naming What She Unnames handout.

■ *Discussion/building connections*: Reconfigure the class into jigsaw groups comprising students who each focused on a different lens in their original group. Have students compare their readings and complete the remaining columns of their Naming What She Unnames record sheet.

■ *Writing*: Ask students to write a brief journal entry in response to the question, *Which of these perspectives seemed to work the best in terms of your own understanding of the story?*

Naming What She Unnames

Consider the story "She Unnames Them" from the perspective of the three theories listed in the chart on the following page. Use the definitions provided in the Literacy Perspectives Toolkit pp.77-80, as well as your own understanding of each lens. First, each group of three will consider a particular lens. Then new groups of three, each one of whom has read the story from a different perspective, will compare their perspectives. Finally, we will discuss all three perspectives as a whole group.

	Reader Response	Gender	Social Power
What aspects of the story lend themselves to an examination by this particular lens?			
Cite specific textual passages that support this kind of reading.			
If you look through this lens, what themes or patterns in the text are brought into sharper relief?			
If you look through this lens, what questions emerge?			
Do you believe in this reading? why or why not?			

A Final Word

Incorporating literary lenses within Scaffolded Reading Experiences has many benefits. The built-in scaffolding of the SRE makes even the most abstract and complicated literary theory accessible. The rich content of literary theory adds interest and texture to the lessons. By combining lenses and SREs, secondary teachers can teach challenging literature lessons and reading skills at the same time.

CHAPTER 5

Comprehensive SREs for English Classes

Jeff has been teaching secondary English for fifteen years. Although he loves his job more than ever, this year has brought some additional challenges. Like every public school teacher in the country, Jeff feels the pressure of standardized tests, initially ramped up by No Child Left Behind and seemingly not going away any time soon. While confident in his ability to teach reading and writing skills, Jeff knows that he doesn't offer his students much practice in reading informational texts. After all, he tells himself, he became an English teacher because he loves literature. Yet both the standardized tests and the Common Core Standards emphasize the importance of reading informational texts. In addition, for whatever reason, the range of reading abilities in his tenth-grade "regular" students seems to be greater than ever. For purposes of unity of experience, and frankly, clarity of planning, Jeff wants to continue to have the whole class read a single text, but he also wants to make certain he reaches all of his students. After brainstorming a tenth-grade interdisciplinary unit on contemporary issues with his social studies colleague, he decides to tackle the

Universal Declaration of Human Rights, which he thinks is a perfect text for a Scaffolded Reading Experience. He presents the following SRE, modified from one created by Patricia Avery, a social studies professor at the University of Minnesota.

COMPREHENSIVE SRE FOR THE UNIVERSAL DECLARATION OF HUMAN RIGHTS

Introduction: In 1948, largely in response to the horrors of World War II, the United Nations adopted the Universal Declaration of Human Rights (UDHR). The UDHR borrows heavily from the U.S. Bill of Rights, and thus the document should seem at least somewhat familiar to American students. But the UDHR differs from and goes beyond the U.S. Bill of Rights. Considering the two documents and how they differ gives students an opportunity to do some close reading and critical thinking on some extremely important issues.

Selection: Universal Declaration of Human Rights (NY: UN Department of Public Information, 1948; also available online at www.un.org/Overview/rights.html). The Universal Declaration of Human Rights is policy statement adopted by the United Nations General Assembly on December 10, 1948. The document enumerates thirty rights everyone should have, regardless of where he or she lives. While modeled in many ways on the U.S. Bill of Rights—which focuses on individual civil and political rights—the UDHR encompasses both individual civil and political rights and collective social, economic, and cultural rights.

Students: High school students of varying abilities in English and social studies classes.

Objectives: To introduce students to the concept of human rights, to help students analyze a primary source document related to human rights, and to help students understand that human rights issues transcend time and place.

THE SRE AT A GLANCE

Prereading Activities	During–Reading Activities	Postreading Activities
Day 1 • Relating the reading to students' lives • Activating background knowledge	None	None

Day 2 • Providing text-specific knowledge • Preteaching vocabulary • Setting direction	• Guided reading	None
Day 3 None	None	• Discussion • Building connections
Day 4 None	None	• Drama • Outreach activities

DAY 1

PREREADING ACTIVITIES

1. *Relating the reading to students' lives* (25 minutes)

- Begin by asking students to think of situations in which an individual or a group has been denied fundamental rights. These may include times the students themselves have felt deprived of their rights. You may want to give examples, such as African Americans being denied the right to vote during the first half of the twentieth century, or, at the individual level, a person having his or her billfold stolen (the right to be secure).

- Tell students to write a very brief description of this violation on a sheet of paper. Give students an opportunity to share with a classmate sitting close to them. (Some students may not feel comfortable sharing this information; if so they should not be forced to.)

- Ask for volunteers to share with the whole class.

- List on the board the rights that have been violated.

- After you have a good list (approximately ten rights), review the list with the class:

  ▶ Are some of the rights more important than others?

  ▶ Should everyone be entitled to each of these rights? Why?

  ▶ Which rights are essential? What are the consequences when people are denied these rights? (Lead students toward a concept of natural law—that humans are essentially born good, and thereby inherit certain fundamental rights at birth.)

2. *Activating background knowledge* (35 minutes)

In this activity, you will find out what your class knows (or doesn't know) about human rights by creating a class concept map.

- Tell students that for the next few days they will be studying a set of *human rights*— rights most nations and people consider basic rights humans are born with.

(continues)

(continued)

■ Give each student three large note cards. Tell the class to write the first three words, phrases, people, ideas, or the like that come to mind when they think of human rights, one on each card. (Tell them to write in large letters and use a pen or marker.)

■ Ask students, five or six at a time, to tape their note cards to a classroom wall, grouping identical cards together. Students should also group words or phrases they think are similar and form a category. For example, *Nelson Mandela, Mahatma Gandhi,* and *Martin Luther King, Jr.* might be grouped together because they were all advocates for human rights. Words such as *freedom, liberty,* and *justice* might be grouped together because they are principles or values associated with human rights.

■ At this point, you might create a concept map like that shown in the figure, or you can simply continue to work from the students' note cards.

■ After all students have placed their note cards on the wall, ask these questions:

  ▶ Do you see words and phrases that go together and form a category? (Some categories may already be evident.)

  ▶ What label might you give this group of words/phrases to show how it is related to human rights? (For example, the label *violations* might be given to words and phrases such as *torture, child abuse, murder, slavery,* and *stealing.*)

  ▶ As you look at our concept map, what observations can you make about what we know about human rights? (Students may notice that their concept maps tend to focus on the negatives, or that most of their examples are from the United States.)

Concept Map on Human Rights

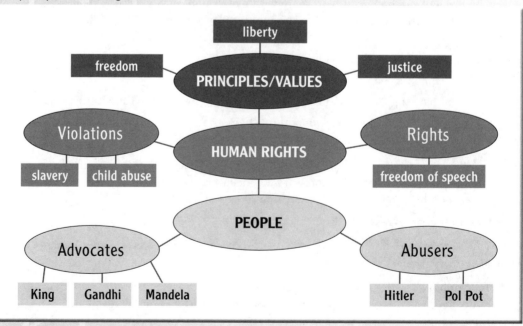

The class concept map lets you determine students' familiarity with the topic. It is quite likely that no one will have thought of the United Nations or the Universal Declaration of Human Rights. If someone has, use that as a bridge to reading the document. Regardless, acknowledge what the students know about human rights and tell them that they will be learning more about them. More specifically, they will focus on a document created by the United Nations nearly sixty years ago that stipulates that all persons should have certain rights simply because they are human. This document is the Universal Declaration of Human Rights.

DAY 2

PREREADING ACTIVITIES

1. *Providing text-specific knowledge* (10 minutes)

   ■ Present students with a fairly detailed preview of the UDHR, including an overview of the content as well as basic information about the context in which the document was written. Address any questions students may ask.

2. *Preteaching vocabulary* (5 minutes)

   ■ A few words and phrases in the UDHR (such as *inalienable rights, asylum,* and *tribunal*) may be unfamiliar to students. Present the words in context and ask whether anyone knows or can infer the definition of each word. Correct or supplement students' definitions so that students end up with complete and accurate definitions.

3. *Setting direction* (10 minutes)

   ■ Ask students to complete one of the reading guides shown in the next figures as they read the document. All the information needed to respond to reading guide 1 is in the document. However, to correctly respond to reading guide 2, students need to have some familiarity with the U.S. Bill of Rights. Since students who have only recently immigrated to the United States may not have this knowledge, they should be asked to complete reading guide 1.

DURING-READING ACTIVITIES

Guided reading (25 minutes)

   ■ Students should complete one of the reading guides as they silently read UDHR.

(continued)

Reading Guide 1: Categorizing Human Rights as Civil or Political Versus Social, Economic, or Cultural

Civil or Political Rights	Social, Economic, or Cultural Rights

Reading Guide 2: How Are the Rights Listed in the Universal Declaration of Human Rights and the U.S. Bill of
Rights Similar and Different?

Rights Listed in the UDHR and the U.S. Bill of Rights	Rights Listed Only in the UDHR

(continues)

(continued)

DAY 3

POSTREADING ACTIVITIES

1. *Discussion* (40 minutes)

- Ask students to share their responses to the reading guides.
- Guide students to an understanding that the U.S. Bill of Rights had an important influence on the development of the UDHR by asking:
  - ▸ What similarities do you see between the U.S. Bill of Rights and the UDHR?
  - ▸ When was each created?
  - ▸ What does this tell you about the relationship between the two?
- When information from both of the guides has been compiled, ask students what observations they can make about the data, ensuring that these points are made:
  - ▸ Most of the rights in the U.S. Bill of Rights are civil and political rights. The U.S. Bill of Rights does not devote much attention to social, economic, or cultural rights. How do students explain this?
  - ▸ "Rugged individualism" and "the work ethic" are strong themes in American life, and these values are often seen to be in opposition to government guarantees of social and economic rights, such as the right to a job or the right to shelter. The fact that some social, economic, and cultural rights are included in UDHR, however, suggests that some nations and peoples value such rights.
  - ▸ There are many violations of these rights throughout the world. Of what significance is a document espousing human rights if the countries of the world do not abide by them? This is an excellent opportunity to talk about the relationship between principles and practice. Principles usually state the behavior and attitudes we think are best (e.g., school mottoes or mission statements, marriage vows). As humans, we often fall short of our principles in practice. But our principles remind us of the ideal.

2. *Building connections* (10 minutes)

At this point, students are ready to use UDHR as a framework for thinking about past and current events.

- Ask students to bring in newspaper articles that show human rights either denied or affirmed. (Bring in several articles as examples; be sure to include some articles that affirm human rights.)
- Have students, using your articles and the articles they have brought in, build a collage of human rights on a wall in your classroom.

DAY 4
POSTREADING ACTIVITIES

1. *Drama* (30 minutes)

- As students bring in their newspaper articles, have them dramatize the right that is affirmed or denied.
- Have students who are observing the enactment identify the right that is being affirmed/denied and speculate about the significance of the right (What would be the consequences if large groups of people were denied this right? How are our lives different because people do have this right?).

2. *Outreach activities* (time as appropriate)

These activities are optional. The time necessary for them varies considerably.

- Ask students how they might promote human rights within their school or community and if any of them would like to participate in such activities. Support those that do and give them credit as your time and course requirements allow.
- Some students might want to educate others about human rights issues. Of course, also support students that choose this activity as your time and circumstances allow.

Jeff's assessment of the SRE on the Universal Declaration of Human Rights was that it provided a rich and robust reading experience for all of his students, regardless of their reading abilities. Based on this, he decided to develop an SRE for one of his favorite contemporary short stories, "The Boy Without a Flag." Ever mindful of his increasingly diverse student population, Jeff has worked hard to diversify his curriculum, including more writers of color who focus on issues of contemporary urban life. Given the issue of citizenship and human rights inherent in the story about a young Puerto Rican boy who feels disenfranchised, Jeff decided this piece of fiction would be a perfect complement to the SRE on the informational text, the UDHR, that he just completed. In fact, he's talked his social studies colleague into trying out this story as well. Following is Jeff's complete SRE for "The Boy Without a Flag."

COMPREHENSIVE SRE FOR "THE BOY WITHOUT A FLAG" BY ABRAHAM RODRIGUEZ, JR.

Introduction: "What does it mean to pledge allegiance to the flag of the United States of America? Why is the recitation of the pledge such a controversial topic? What does it mean to stand up for what you believe? Do you have the courage to stand up for your convictions even in the face of extreme pressure from peers, teachers, and parents? Has an adult that you admired, even your parents, ever let you down?"

These are among the many issues that surface in the short story, "The Boy Without a Flag" by Abraham Rodriguez, Jr. This interdisciplinary SRE unit can be used in language arts, social studies, or humanities classes. It is designed to encourage students to analyze current events and develop their own positions on a controversial issue.

Selection: "The Boy Without a Flag" is a short story by the contemporary Latino writer Abraham Rodriguez, Jr. The story is written in very accessible language. The protagonist is a young Puerto Rican boy who refuses to join his class in the recitation of the Pledge of Allegiance because he believes his father does not want him to. When the boy is sent to the principal's office, he is surprised to learn that his father is ashamed rather than proud of his defiance. This leaves the boy feeling caught between the culture of school and the culture of home. He is, indeed, a "boy without a flag."

Students: Students in grades 9–12 in either language arts or social studies classes. This SRE is particularly appropriate in diverse classrooms.

Objectives: To understand the conflict of values presented in the story, understand the dynamics of the parent-child relationship presented in the story, relate the conflicts presented in the story to current events, and analyze the issues undergirding themes of citizenship and democracy.

THE SRE AT A GLANCE

Prereading Activities	During–Reading Activities	Postreading Activities
Day 1 • Relating the reading to students' lives • Activating background knowledge • Providing text-specific knowledge	None	None

Day 2 • Building Connections • Preteaching vocabulary • Setting direction	• Guided reading	None
Day 3 None	None	• Discussion

DAY 1

PREREADING ACTIVITIES

1. *Relating the reading to students' lives and activating background knowledge* (**25 minutes**)

- Tell students they will be reading a story about a boy who refuses to stand and recite the Pledge of Allegiance. Ask them what they remember about reciting the pledge in elementary school. Discuss current debates about the pledge at both the national and local level. (*ten minutes*)

- Have students complete a close reading of the Pledge of Allegiance in groups. (*fifteen minutes*)

2. *Providing text-specific knowledge* (**30 minutes**)

- Break students into groups of three or four, and distribute the pledge handout shown on p. 98.

- Ask students to paraphrase the pledge and answer specific questions about it.

- Have students write a new pledge that everyone can recite.

- Circulate and provide guidance as students work.

- Have a spokesperson from each group recite the group's pledge. Ask group members to explain how their pledge takes into account something the original doesn't. Some students may have retained the pledge in the original form, and if some did they should explain why.

DAY 2

PREREADING ACTIVITIES

Building connections, preteaching vocabulary, setting direction (**20 minutes**)

- Create a strip poem:
  - ▶ Pass out strips of colored paper. Tell students that the name of the story they will be reading is "The Boy Without a Flag." Ask them to write, "I am the [girl/boy] without a _____."

(continues)

(continued)

Pledge of Allegiance Handout

> **I pledge allegiance to the flag**
> **of the United States of America**
> **and to the republic for which it stands,**
> **one nation under God, indivisible,**
> **with liberty and justice for all.**

The Boy Without a Flag

Read or recite the pledge in your group, either together or individually.

Is there anything you don't like about reciting the pledge? Be honest.

Restate the pledge in your own words. Use your normal everyday language.

Who might not be able to recite the pledge comfortably as it is written?

Pretend you're a group of newly elected Congressional lawmakers. Your goal is to write a pledge that most U.S. citizens would feel comfortable reciting—and one that would survive over time. Think about the purpose of your pledge as well as key concepts you want to convey and the words that will best do so.

Write your pledge here.

    ▸ Collect the strips and read them aloud as a poem.

■ Have students quickwrite to the following prompt: *What do you remember about the atmosphere of your elementary school?*

    ▸ Ask students to close their eyes and try to think back to what their fifth- or sixth-grade classroom was like. Ask them to try to remember any schoolwide programs in the auditorium.

    ▸ Give them colored index cards and ask them to write two or three words they thought of. Pick two recorders and have them write the words on the board as their classmates volunteer them.

    ▸ Discuss the overall impressions made by the words. Are they positive or negative?

DURING-READING ACTIVITIES

Guided reading (35 minutes)

■ Read the first five pages of the story aloud.

■ Pass out copies of the story map. Model answering the first five questions.

"The Boy Without a Flag" Story Map

Story maps are questions and things to think about that when taken all together guide you through the story. The prompts help you anticipate where you are going as well as remind you of where you have been. **For this story map, it's a good idea to work with one or two other students. As you read, make sure you mark up your text with questions or comments!** For example:

- Annotate the text in the margins of the document.
- Ask questions about the characters, the author, or things you don't understand.
- Underline key passages and phrases and write interpretations.
- Look for various writing techniques the author uses, and note or highlight them.
- Write/highlight main points about the story.

Read pages 11–17:

1. Who is telling the story? How old do you think he is? What grade do you think he is in?

2. What do you notice about the author's style of writing?

(continues)

(continued)

3. What grade school memories does this story make you think of?

4. Since this story really isn't about Miss Colon's love life, why do you think the author included details about it?

5. The story changes gears on page 16, switching from school to the narrator's thoughts about his father. What do you learn about their relationship?

Read pages 17–23 (to the end of the first paragraph):

6. The setting switches back to the school auditorium here. Why did the author insert all that stuff about the father instead of writing the story in a more normal or linear way?

7. Why didn't the boy stand up for the Pledge of Allegiance? What is your opinion about this?

8. What is the response of Miss Colon and Mr. Rios? What are some conflicts you've had with your teachers? Were they based on principle? When were you sure that you were right and they were wrong, or did you decide otherwise?

9. What is respect? Why does Mr. Rios say that the boy doesn't have respect? Do you agree?

10. How do you think the father will react when he learns about his son's actions? Why?

Read Pages 23–30:

11. The narrator has images that "attack him at night." What's causing the anxiety he's feeling?

12. Why is it so important to the adults that the narrator salutes the flag? What's really at stake here?

13. Read the interaction with the principal on page 26 very carefully. What is the most disturbing thing about it?

14. Why doesn't the father stick up for the son?

15. Respond to this quotation on page 27: "My father, my creator, renouncing his creation, repentant."

16. Who is The Enemy? Who is yours?

17. With your partner, underline what you think is the most important sentence in the story.

■ Have students, in pairs or trios, finish reading the story using the story map. At least one student in each pair or group should be able to read well aloud. Point out that the story map asks them to read five pages at a time and then answer questions.

■ For homework, ask students who didn't get to the end of the story or complete the story map to do so before class tomorrow.

DAY 3
POSTREADING ACTIVITIES

Discussion (45 minutes)

■ Lead a whole-class discussion/recap of the story. Give students a few minutes to rejoin their reading partners. Ask them to underline or highlight what they believe is the most important sentence of the story. Then ask each pair or trio from Day 3 to read their chosen sentence. Discuss what elements of the story were highlighted or underscored by the choice of sentences. *(ten minutes)*

■ Ask, "Should the father have supported the son in his decision not to recite the pledge?" Have students line up at the front of the room, those who strongly believe the father should have supported his son on one end, those who strongly believe the father did the right thing by acquiescing to school officials on the other, those who feel neutral in the middle. Ask students from each location to defend their position. *(15 minutes)*

■ Discussion web: Should students be required to recite the Pledge of Allegiance? *(20 minutes)*

  ▸ Have students follow the directions on the discussion web handout on p. 102. This activity brings the discussion of the story back full circle.

  ▸ If students have already fully discussed the pledge, prepare a discussion web on another topic (for example: "Should parents always support their children?" "Is obedience a virtue?").

Directions for the Discussion Web

1. **With a partner, discuss the pros and cons of requiring students to recite the Pledge of Allegiance. You might want to take into account recent local, state, and national events.**

2. **Jot down reasons for both positions in the yes and no columns. You need to jot down only key words or phrases.**

3. **Join with another pair of classmates and try to reach a consensus on this issue. Your goal is to come up with a group conclusion, even though some members may disagree with that conclusion.**

4. **Select a spokesperson to present your group's view to the rest of the class. Have him or her report the best reason for your position.**

(continues)

(continued)

The Discussion Web

DISCUSSION WEB FOR "THE BOY WITHOUT A FLAG"

Reasons

NO   Should students be required to recite the Pledge of Allegiance?   YES

Conclusion

A Final Word

So there you have it—two complete SREs—one for a challenging and historically important document with which students need to become familiar and one for a contemporary short story that at least on the surface is not likely to be difficult for most students. Why have we built SREs around these two selections? The answer is different for each.

The Universal Declaration of Human Rights is not something students are likely to pick up on their own or even know about unless someone, most likely a teacher, brings it to their attention. Students need to be motivated to read it, they need to appreciate the difficulty the United Nations had in crafting and getting approval for such a document, and they need to understand the importance of human rights. The struggle for human rights is a continuing one. It is as relevant today as it was sixty years ago and will continue to be relevant and vitally important in the future.

"The Boy Without a Flag," on the other hand, is a story students might well pick up on their own, find interesting, and be motivated to read independently. The central issue with this text, the central purpose of our SRE, is to help students see beyond the surface of the story and understand the conflict of values it presents, recognize the dynamics of the parent-child relationship it depicts, consider how the conflicts in the story relate to the real world and their own lives, and investigate important themes in some depth. Not many students would deal with these sorts of understandings, considerations, and investigations without the scaffolding provided by the SRE.

We also want to note that including these two SREs as we near the end of this book allows us to once again stress that SREs are appropriate for exposition as well as for fiction, to again show that SREs can be effective for both fairly easy and challenging texts, to again demonstrate that different texts and different purpose require quite different SREs.

CHAPTER 6

Selecting Texts and Assessing Student Performance

There are two final considerations as you prepare to incorporate SREs into your own classroom. The first is selecting texts; as all experienced teachers know, the most critical element of your instructional design is your text. The second, logically and inevitably, is using strategies for student assessment.

Selecting Texts

If the mantra for real estate is "location, location, location," then the mantra for success with SREs should be "selection, selection, selection." While it's absolutely true that one of the primary advantages of SREs is their ability to make a difficult text more comprehensible, it is also true that no instructional design can turn a poorly written or truly inaccessible text into an enjoyable

It is also true that no instructional design can turn a poorly written or truly inaccessible text into an enjoyable and informative reading experience.

and informative reading experience. There are several factors to consider as you select texts around which to develop SREs: genre, relationship to the curriculum, topical interest, background knowledge required, readability and difficulty, and sources. Additionally, it is important to consider the influence that the Common Core State Standards initiative is likely to exert on text selection.

What Genre Should Students Read?

The beauty of SREs is that they work equally well with fiction, nonfiction, and poetry. Take a mental inventory of the kinds of texts you tend to read with your students. If you are like most English teachers, you probably favor fiction. Let us make a case for the other two.

The Common Core State Standards call for all students to be able to read, comprehend, and analyze all types of texts, nonfiction and poetry included. Secondary students often find poetry difficult or inaccessible (Travers 1984). By offering motivating prereading activities, scaffolded while-reading activities, and structured postreading discussion and writing opportunities, SREs help students comprehend, interpret, and appreciate poetry. Nonfiction is an increasingly important component of the language arts curriculum. The passages on most state and national assessments and standardized tests are nonfiction, so it's essential that your students know how to make meaning from such texts. Additionally, the ability to understand nonfiction texts is essential in our increasingly complex world of print and information.

The ability to understand nonfiction texts is essential in our increasingly complex world of print and information.

Relationship to the Curriculum

You also need to consider where the selection fits into your curriculum. An SRE can be an excellent way to introduce a longer text or assignment. For example, the "The Boy Without a Flag" SRE (see Chapter 5) could be an introductory activity for Abraham Rodriguez's novel *Spidertown*, or *When I Was Puerto Rican*, by Esmeralda Santiago. An SRE can be a concluding activity, too. The Universal Declaration of Human Rights SRE could serve as a concluding activity after students have read several speeches and essays by leaders like Gandhi, Martin Luther King, Jr., and Nelson Mandela.

SREs are also an effective way to focus on particular reading and comprehension skills without making this seem like decontextualized test prep. Well-structured SREs give students the skills and experience they need to navigate difficult informational text wherever they encounter it.

Topical Interest

One of the most obvious yet important criteria in selecting texts for SREs is students' inherent interest in the subject. In *Reading Don't Fix No Chevies* (2002), Smith and Wilhelm argue that inherent interest is necessary to motivate young readers, especially boys. You don't have to pander to students' interests, basing your lessons only on popular culture or student hobbies. Rather, select texts that have a vital, natural connection to students' interests and lives. For example, a seemingly dry informational text about social networking could connect to students' activities on Facebook and other social networks. Articles or stories about animals or pets have a natural hook, as do narratives and nonfiction texts about the complexity of human relationships. The SRE on the Universal Declaration of Human Rights connects directly to contemporary issues that affect students' lives.

Select texts that have a vital, natural connection to students' interests and lives.

Required Background Knowledge

An SRE can and should build on students' background knowledge. Reading better and smarter is hugely more difficult—impossible, some would argue—if a student has *no* background knowledge on which to build. Many technical texts, especially from the sciences and social sciences, require some basic background knowledge for a reader to be able to enter the text. Without some mechanism to activate prior knowledge, readers will be frustrated and are very likely to fail.

In deciding which texts require an appropriate level of background knowledge, consider what prior experience students may have had with the topic. This will, of course, vary, depending on your overall school curriculum, your students' developmental level, and their reading experiences to date.

Using shorter texts also helps you monitor how well students are reading the selection and where they might be experiencing difficulty.

Readability and Difficulty

You'll also need to consider some specific text characteristics, like length, vocabulary, and sentence structure (Graves and Graves 2003).

Working with shorter pieces is particularly effective with less skilled and less motivated readers; they can experience the entire instructional sequence in three or four days. Using shorter texts also helps you monitor how well students are reading the selection and where they might be experiencing difficulty.

Vocabulary is one of the central factors related to text difficulty. Vocabulary can be pretaught as part of an SRE, and building students' vocabularies is an essential part of improving their ability to read better and smarter. On the other hand, if a large proportion of the words in a text need to be defined, that text is probably too difficult.

Similarly, sentence structure greatly affects accessibility. Overly long or complex sentences may make it difficult for your students to read and comprehend a selection. Such sentences may also seriously undercut students' motivation, perhaps preventing struggling readers from even trying.

Overall Quality of the Writing

As an expert reader and teacher, you know that there are texts that seem to hook readers immediately and others that are more difficult to enter. Texts for adolescents should not be like bad-tasting medicine—distasteful in the moment but good for them in the long run. The writing style of the texts you offer your students should be appealing—inviting, interesting, accessible, clear, easy to follow, full of vitality. While we all eventually encounter texts we have to read but don't necessarily enjoy, when developing SREs find texts with an engaging style.

Intended Audience

As you add informational texts to your curriculum, you will be culling texts from a wide variety of sources, many of them not intended for adolescent readers. The following questions will help you determine whether the text is appropriate for your students:

- **Does this text assume life experience that my students have not yet had?**
- **Does this text make assumptions about background knowledge that my students don't possess?**
- **Does this text make allusions to things with which my students are not familiar?**
- **Is the content age-appropriate?**
- **Does the text make social/cultural assumptions about its audience that don't apply to my students?**
- **Is the text a good developmental match for my students, considering their grade level, life experiences, school experiences, and overall reading ability?**

Sources

We've discussed quite a few criteria for texts that are compatible with the SRE approach. How should you go about finding them? Where should you look?

Begin with what you already have. Your curriculum is filled with short stories, essays, and poems that you might teach differently with an SRE.

Begin with what you already have. Your curriculum is filled with short stories, essays, and poems that you might teach differently with an SRE. You might even reclaim selections you've previously dismissed as too difficult—a Scaffolded Reading Experience allows your students to read texts they couldn't have before.

Also, make better use of the ubiquitous literature anthology. Increasingly, the language arts textbooks that weigh down your bookshelves and your students' backpacks are filled with short fiction, poems, and informational texts. Although the teaching guides that accompany these texts do not provide the complete scaffolded experiences described in this book, the anthologies themselves remain an excellent source for a variety of material.

Other sources for appropriate texts are *The Best American Nonrequired Reading* (Eggers 2010), *The Best American Essays* (Hitchins 2010), *The Best American Short Stories* (Russo 2010), and *Good Poems* (Keillor 2003). There are also very cool collections of "sudden fiction"—short-short stories ideal for an SRE. Poetry sites such as www.poetry.org are a rich repository of poems.

The language arts textbooks that weigh down your bookshelves and your students' backpacks are filled with short fiction, poems, and informational texts.

Contemporary newspapers, magazines, and journals are great sources of short essays and articles. *National Geographic* and *Scientific American* are surprisingly rich sources for informational texts. Local and national newspapers are an excellent source for opinion pieces and editorials. One could even build an SRE around a recipe.

Finally, there is an abundance (some might say a surfeit) of textual material online. Essays, political articles, editorials, blogs, and 'zines abound. You might even create an SRE that requires a critical reading of a Wikipedia entry. Although extra caution needs to be taken when assessing the reliability, validity, and appropriateness of online sources, an added benefit of using these sources is that you will make your students better, smarter surfers of the Internet as well as better, smarter readers!

Likely Influence of the Common Core State Standards Initiative

As noted in the Common Core State Standards mission statement, the Standards are designed to provide

> a consistent, clear understanding of what students are expected to learn, so teachers and parents know what they need to do to help them. The standards are designed to be robust and relevant to the real world, reflecting the knowledge and skills that our young people need for success in college and careers. With American students fully prepared for the future, our communities will be best positioned to compete successfully in the global economy. (www.corestandares.org)

In other words, the Standards press toward all students learning much the same content and toward this content being challenging. Much more information on the Standards is available on the website listed above. But what this means for selecting texts is that there is likely to be increasing pressure to select challenging texts for all or at least most students (Adams 2010–11), and that many students are going to need substantial support to successfully read and learn from those texts.

Assessing Student Performance

There are a number of purposes for assessing students and a variety of audiences for those assessments. We assess in order to evaluate individual students, schools, districts, and states; provide students, parents, schools, districts, and taxpayers with information on students' accomplishments and shortcomings; and evaluate and better understand our instruction so that we can improve it. Our focus here is on assessment for the purpose of improving instruction. Such assessments tend to be informal, teacher-made, subjective, and specific to what is being taught.

The central question is, how well are your students dealing with the literary selections they are reading in your classes, particularly those they are reading with the assistance of SREs? In answering this question, you need to consider students':

- **Motivation, interests, and attitudes**
- **Comprehension and appreciation**
- **Understanding of literary concepts and devices**

You can do this through three types of assessments: observing, discussion and questioning, and testing. This approach is informed by a number of testing authorities, including Afflerbach (2007), Johnston (1997), Wiggins (1999), Wilson and Calfee (2011), Beck and McKeown (1981), and Pitcher et al. (2007).

Observing

As the anthropologist Ashley Montagu once observed, "If you want to know what people believe, don't read what they write, don't ask them what they believe, just observe what they do." Observation is certainly one of the most powerful and revealing approaches to assessment, particularly when considering motivation, interests, and attitudes. Questions that can be answered, or at least partially answered, by observing your students include:

Observation is certainly one of the most powerful and revealing approaches to assessment.

- What are their general attitudes toward reading? Do they carry around books they are reading on their own? Do they discuss books with one another? Do they ask you about books they might read or tell you about what they're reading?

- What are their attitudes toward learning? Do they come to class on time? Do they settle down to work relatively soon? Do they seem to look forward to the class? Are they attentive and courteous to you and to their classmates?

- What are their attitudes toward the literature you read in class? Do they seem to look forward to reading the selections? Do they seem to enjoy reading them? Are they on task when they are reading in class? Do they complete out-of-class reading assignments?

- What are their attitudes toward the SREs? Do they seem to welcome them? Do they pay attention during your presentations? Do they complete the activities?

Positive answers to these questions are a good indication that your students are responding well to your class, the selections they read, and the SREs you use to support their reading. Of course, not all students nor all questions result in the same answers. If there are a significant number of negative responses, it makes good sense to consider some changes in the overall organization and functioning of the class, in the selections you choose, or in the frequency and nature of the SREs you use.

Discussion and Questioning

While observation can be one of the most powerful forms of assessment, it's by nature less focused than discussion and questioning in which you directly probe students about the issues you want to investigate. These more direct approaches are often also more useful than observing for targeting cognitive rather than affective matters.

Discussion and questioning allow you to explore questions such as:

- Do students have the background knowledge to understand the upcoming selection fully? For example, what do students who are about to read *Slaughterhouse-Five* know about World War II, the bombing of Dresden, and the controversy over that bombing? Equally important to understanding and appreciating the novel, how much do they care about these events?

- How much did students learn from their reading? Can they summarize the main events, note important details, or discuss major themes?

- Do students understand the literary devices used in the selection? For example, after reading *The Color Purple,* do they understand the irony that Sofia's independence and need to be her own person is a major factor preventing her from leading an independent life?

- How do students feel about the scaffolding they receive from SREs? Do students appreciate having previews of upcoming selections or would they prefer to read without the information previews provide?

Although discussion and questioning are often more useful than observation for getting at cognitive matters, this doesn't mean they can't be useful for assessing affective concerns like motivation. Pitcher and her colleagues (2007) have developed and tested an inventory for assessing adolescents' motivation to read. Here are just a few of the items:

- **Reading a book is something I like to do**

  __never

  ___not very often

  ___sometimes

  ___often

- **When I am reading a book by myself, I understand**

  ___almost everything I read

  ___some of what I read

  ___almost none of what I read

  ___none of what I read

- **When my teacher asks me a question about what I have read, I**

  ___ can never think of an answer

  ___have trouble thinking of an answer

  ___sometimes think of an answer

  ___always think of an answer

- **When someone gives me a book for a present, I feel**

  ___very happy

  ___sort of happy

  ___sort of unhappy

The inventory includes twenty items, takes about ten minutes to complete, has been tested in a variety of settings, and is included in its entirety in the article.

You can use the Pitcher inventory as presented or modify it to include questions on SREs that are better suited to your classes and concerns. For example, you might include such questions as:

- **I think it is helpful to include SREs for**

    ___**all the selections we read**

    ___**any selections that are at all difficult**

    ___**any selections that are very difficult**

- **The SREs that we have had in class so far are**

    ___**about the right length**

    ___**too short**

    ___**too long**

Similar questions and ones that probe students' feelings in more depth can also be asked orally. Pitcher and her colleagues also include a detailed set of interview questions geared toward adolescents' motivation to read.

Testing

While we think both observation and discussion/questioning are very useful, we believe the most valuable tool for assessing the effects of SREs is a teacher-made test called a story map. It was originally suggested by Beck and McKeown (1981) and its use has been researched by Liang, Watkins, Graves, and Hosp (2010).

A story map comprises two sets of questions on a reading selection. The first set—the story map proper—is about a dozen questions that get at the essence of the story. They deal with the major events and themes and follow the chronology from beginning to end. Both literal and inferential questions are included, although most are likely to be literal. Students' answers to these questions demonstrate whether they have a basic understanding of the text.

We believe the most valuable tool for assessing the effects of SREs is a teacher-made test called a story map.

The second set is two or three extension questions that ask students to go beyond the selection. They typically require students to relate the selection to their lives or other selections they have read, make judgments about the text or its author, and comment on formal (structural) or literary aspects of the text. These questions almost always involve inferences.

The next figures are story maps (pp.114–115). The first, designed for middle-grade students, was created by Sally Goddard, a teacher in the St. Louis Park, Minnesota, public schools. The second, designed for high school students, was created by Lauren Liang, formerly a middle-grade teacher and now on the faculty at the University of Utah.

Several aspects of these story maps warrant comment. First, they demonstrate that a relatively small number of well-chosen questions can get at the essence of a story and do a good job of revealing students' understanding. Second, some of the questions—question 1 on *Holes* (p. 114) and questions 1 and 2 on "Silk Stockings" (p. 115), for example—use a technique called *fronting*, in which a brief statement points students to the part of the selection the question focuses on ("Stanley Yelnats was sent to Camp Green Lake, a boy's detention center). Third, several other questions—questions 2 and 3 in *Holes* and questions 5 and 6 in "Silk Stockings," for example—use a *stacking* technique, in which closely related questions are grouped together. This means fewer numbered questions, which students see as a good thing!

Students can respond to story-map questions in a number of ways. One possibility is for each student to write out the answers to the questions and hand them in. This probably gives you the most information, but it takes a lot of your time. Another possibility is for each student to write out the answers to the questions, pair with a partner for one-on-one feedback, then review the questions as a class. A third possibility is for students to work on the questions in groups, after which each group reports to the class on a subset of the questions.

STORY MAP FOR LOUIS SACHAR'S *HOLES*

1. Stanley Yelnats was sent to Camp Green Lake, a boy's detention center. To what did Stanley's family always attribute their bad luck?

2. What did the boys at Camp Green Lake need to do every day as punishment? How did they deal with this punishment?

3. Stanley became friends with some of the other boys at Camp Green Lake. Everyone had a nickname. What were some of the nicknames? Did the nicknames fit? For example, why was Stanley called Caveman? How did this nickname change the way Stanley felt about himself?

4. How would you describe the adults that worked at Camp Green Lake (Mr. Pendanski, Mr. Sir, the Warden)? Why would people like this choose to have a job working with troubled boys?

5. What does Stanley dig up in a hole that the warden finds so interesting? Do the boys realize that the warden is now looking for something particular in these holes?

6. When Zero hits Mr. Pendanski with a shovel and then heads out into the desert, what does everyone think will happen to him?

7. After Stanley finds Zero, they have many discussions as they try to survive in the desert. What coincidences do they experience between their present lives and their family's history?

8. How do Stanley and Zero start to change on their journey together?

9. What mystery do Stanley and Zero solve when they are out in the desert? What do they decide to do about it?

10. How are Stanley's and Zero's lives different at the end of the story?

Extension Questions

1. *Holes* is made up of two different stories: Stanley's experience at Camp Green Lake and the tall tale of his great-great-grandfather in the Wild West. How does the author, Louis Sachar, tell the stories and switch between them? How does he connect the two stories at the end of the book? Is this an effective writing technique? Why or why not?

2. The warden is a miserable, nasty woman. What is it about her that makes her such an evil character? Think of and share examples of other evil women characters you know from books and movies. How is the warden similar to some of these other female villains?

STORY MAP FOR KATE CHOPIN'S "A PAIR OF SILK STOCKINGS"

1. Mrs. Sommers is the "unexpected possessor of fifteen dollars." How does she intend to spend the money?
2. At the beginning of the story, we are given clues about Mrs. Sommers' typical shopping behavior. What type of shopper is she?
3. What kind of life did Mrs. Sommers lead before she was Mrs. Sommers?
4. Mrs. Sommers sits down at the counter when she comes into the store. Why is she so tired?
5. What does Mrs. Sommers buy first? Does she think about this purchase before making it? What does she do after she purchases the item?
6. What does Mrs. Sommers buy next? What are the clerks' reactions to Mrs. Sommers?
7. What does Mrs. Sommers expect when she enters the restaurant? Why?
8. Mrs. Sommers orders an assortment of food. What is implied when her order is called a "tasty bite"?
9. When Mrs. Sommers goes to the matinee, the narrator states, "There was no one present who bore quite the attitude which Mrs. Sommers did to her surroundings." What does this mean?
10. How does Mrs. Sommers interact with the other theatergoers?

Extension Questions

1. Mrs. Sommers' original plan for spending the money involved her children. Based on this original plan, what are her attitudes toward her children?
2. Using what you know about Kate Chopin's writing and her views on the roles of women, what do you think Chopin's message is in this story?

A Final Word

Armed with an in-depth understanding of SREs, how to select texts, and ways to approach assessment, you will be able to make each and every reading experience a positive one, both for your students and for you. We hope that you will find that incorporating SREs in your classroom will help all of your students become better, smarter readers.

LITERATURE CITED

Agee, J. 1957/1998. *A Death in the Family*. New York: Vintage Books.

Alexander, C. 1998. *The Endurance: Shackleton's Legendary Antarctic Expedition*. New York: Knopf.

Alexi, S. 1994. *The Lone Ranger and Tonto Fistfight in Heaven*. New York: Harper Perennial.

Anaya, R. 1972. *Bless Me, Ultima*. Berkeley, CA: Quinto Sol Publications.

Atwood, M. 1991. "Significant Moments in the Life of My Mother." In *World Masterpieces*, ed. E. Thompson. Englewood Cliffs, NJ: Prentice Hall.

Avi. 1990. *The True Confessions of Charlotte Doyle*. New York: Orchard.

Baldwin, J. 1994. *Sonny's Blues*. Stuttgart, Germany: Klett.

Barry, L. 2002. "Seventh Grade." In *The Good Times Are Killing Me*. Seattle: Sasquatch Books.

Blake, M. 1991. *Dances with Wolves*. New York: Newmarket Press.

Bradbury, R. 1951. *Fahrenheit 451*. New York: Ballantine Books.

Broker, I. 1983. *Night Flying Woman: An Ojibway Narrative*. St. Paul: Minnesota Historical Society.

Brooks, G. 1959. "We Real Cool" in *The Bean Eaters*. New York: Harper & Brothers.

Brooks, M. 2004. *Confessions of a Heartless Girl*. New York: Harper Collins.

Brothers Grimm, "Snow White and the Seven Dwarfs." http://www.literaturecollec tion.com/a/grimm-brothers/549/

Bryson, B. 2006. *The Life and Times of the Thunderbolt Kid: A Memoir*. New York: Broadway Books.

Burns, R. 1998. *The Collected Poems of Robert Burns*. Hertfordshire, England: Wordsworth Editions.

Chaucer, G. 2008. *The Canterbury Tales*. New York: The Modern Library.

Chbosky, S. 1999. *The Perks of Being a Wallflower*. New York: Pocket Books.

Chopin, K. 1987/2002. "A Pair of Silk Stockings." In *Great American Short Stories,* ed. P. Negri, 188–200. Minella, NY: Dover Publications.

Cisneros, S. 1984/2009. *The House on Mango Street*. New York: Vintage Contemporaries.

———. 1991. *Woman Hollering Creek and Other Stories*. New York: Random House.

Collier, E. 1994. *Breeder and Other Stories*. Baltimore: DuForcelf.

Conrad, J. 1902/1986. *Heart of Darkness*. New York: Buccaneer Books.

Cortazar, J. 1944. "House Taken Over" (Casa tomada). *Los anales de Buenos Aires*. Buenos Aires: El Museo.

Crane, S. 1894. *The Red Badge of Courage*. New York: D. Appleton and Company.

Creech, S. 2001. *Love That Dog: A Novel*. New York: Harper Collins.

Curtis, C. P. 1997. *The Watsons Go to Birmingham—1963*. New York: Bantam Doubleday Dell Books for Young Readers.

Edwards, S. 1985. *George Midgett's War*. New York: Scribner.

Eggers D., and D. Sedaris. 2010. *The Best American Nonrequired Reading*. Boston: Mariner Books.

Evan, L. 1988. "Thomas Nast: Political Cartoonist Extraordinaire?" *Cobblestone* 29 (11) November.

Faulkner, W. 1931/2010. "A Rose for Emily." In *The Norton Introduction to Literature,* tenth edition. New York: W. W. Norton & Company.

Fitzgerald, F. S. 1925/1995. *The Great Gatsby*. New York: Scribner Paperback Fiction.

Forbes, E. 1987. *Johnny Tremain*. New York: Yearling.

Forster, E. M. 1956. *Aspects of the Novel*. New York: Harcourt, Brace and World

Frank, A. 1958. *Anne Frank: The Diary of a Young Girl*. New York: Listening Library.

Frazier, C. 2006. *Cold Mountain*. New York: Grove.

Gaines, E. J. 1993. *A Lesson Before Dying*. New York: Knopf.

Giovanni, N. 1968/2003. "Nikki-Rosa." In *The Collected Poetry of Nikki Giovanni*. New York: HarperCollins.

Gladwell, M. 2007. *Blink: The Power of Thinking Without Thinking*. New York: Little Brown and Company.

Harte, F. B. 1960. *The Outcast of Poker Flats and Other Tales*. New York: The New American Library of World Literature.

Hersey, J. 1946. *A Bell for Adano*. New York: The Modern Library.

Hemmingway, E. 1995. *A Farewell to Arms*. New York: Scribner.

Hitchens, C., and R. Atwan. 2010. *The Best American Essays*. Boston: Mariner Books.

Huff, B. 1990. Greening the City Streets. New York: Clarion.

Hughes, L. 1994. "I, Too, Sing America." In *The Collected Poem of Langston Hughes*. New York: Knopf and Vintage Books.

Hurston, Z. N. 1937. *Their Eyes Were Watching God*. Philadelphia: J. B. Lippincott.

Huxley, A. 1932. *Brave New World*. New York: Harper Collins.

Ibsen, H. 1879/1992. *A Doll's House*. Mineola, NY: Dover Publications. Available at http://www.fullbooks.com/A-Doll-s-House.html.

Jiménez, F. 1997. *The Circuit: Stories from the Life of a Migrant Child*. New York: Houghton Mifflin.

Keillor, G. 2003. *Good Poems*. New York: Penguin.

Kieth, S. 2001. *Zero Girl*. La Jolla, CA: DC Comics.

Kipling, R. 2004. *Rikki-Tikki-Tavi: The Jungle Book*. New York: HarperCollins.

Krakauer, J. 1998. *Into Thin Air*. New York: Anchor Books.

Lahiri, J. 2000. *Interpreter of Maladies*. Boston: Houghton Mifflin.

Lawrence, J., and R. E. Lee. 1972. *The Night Thoreau Spent in Jail*. New York: Bantam Books.

Le Guin, U.K. 1994. *Buffalo Gals and Other Animal Presences*. New York: Penguin/Roc.

Lee, H. 1960. *To Kill a Mockingbird*. Woodstalk, IL: Dramatic Publishing.

Lee, L. Y. 1986. "The Gift." In *Rose*. Rochester, NY: BOA Editions.

Lester, L. 1968/2005. *To Be a Slave*. New York: Penguin Group.

Lowry, L. 1989. *Number the Stars*. Second Edition. Boston: Houghton Mifflin.

———. 1993. *The Giver*. Boston: Houghton Mifflin.

MacLachlan, P. 1991. *Journey*. New York: Delacorte.

Márquez, G. G. 1955/1990. "A Very Old Man with Enormous Wings." In *Leaf Storm*. New York: Harper Colophon Books.

Markle, S. 1988. *Science Mini-Mysteries*. New York: Atheneum.

Martel, Y. 2001. *Life of Pi: A Novel*. New York: Harcourt.

Merriam, E. 1964. "How to Eat a Poem." In *It Doesn't Always Have to Rhyme* New York: Atheneum.

Miller, A. 1949. *Death of a Salesman*. New York City: Morosco Theatre.

Morrison, T. 1987. *Beloved*. New York: Knopf.

Myers, W. D. 1999/2001. *Monster*. New York: Armistad.

Myracle, L. 2004. *ttyl*. New York: Abrams, Amulet.

Noyes, A. 1906. "The Highwayman." *Blackwood's Magazine*. Available at http://www.poemhunter.com/poem/the-highwayman/.

O'Brien, T. 1990. "On the Rainy River." In *The Things They Carried: A Work of Fiction*. New York: Random House.

———. 1990. *The Things They Carried*. Boston: Houghton Mifflin.

O'Henry. 1906/2000. "The Gift of the Magi." In *The Four Million*. Amsterdam, The Netherlands: Fredonia Books.

Orwell, G. 1949. *1984*. New York: Harcourt Inc.

Palahniuk, C. 1997. *Fight club*. New York: Henry Holt.

Park, L. S. 2001. *A Single Shard*. New York: Clarion.

Paulsen, G. 1987/1999. *Hatchet*. New York: Scholastic.

Poe, E. A. 1842. "The Masque of the Red Death." *Graham's Magazine*. Available at www.online-literature.com/poe/36/.

———. 1843. "The Tell-Tale Heart." *The Pioneer* January 1:29–31.

———. 1849. "Annabel Lee." *Sartain's Union Magazine*. Available at http://www.poemhunter.com/poem/annabel-lee/.

Rapp, A. 2004. *Under the Wolf, Under the Dog*. Somerville, MA: Candlewick.

Reed, H. 2006. "Naming of Parts." In *Literature: The Human Experience*. Boston: Bedford/St. Martin's.

Remarque, E. 1983. *All Quiet on the Western Front*. Cutchogue, NY: Buccaneer Books.

Rodriguez, A., Jr. 1993. *Spidertown*. New York: Hyperion.

———. 1999. *The Boy Without a Flag: Tales of the South Bronx*. Minneapolis, MN: Milkweed Editions.

Rogasky, B. 2002. *Smoke and Ashes: The Story of the Holocaust*. New York: Holiday House.

Roethke, T. 1948. "My Papa's Waltz." In *The Lost Son and Other Poems*. New York: Doubleday.

Russo, R., and H. Pitlor. 2010. *The Best American Short Stories*. Boston: Mariner Books.

Sachar, L. 1998. *Holes*. New York: Farrar, Straus and Giroux.

Sanburg, C. 1916. "Fog." *Chicago Poems*. New York: Henry Holt. Available at http://www.bartleby.com/104/76.html.

Santiago, E. 2006. *When I Was Puerto Rican*. Cambridge, MA: De Capo.

Sasaki, R. 1991. "Independence." In *The Loom and Other Stories*. Minneapolis: Greywolf Press.

Satrapi, M. 2000. *Persepolis*. New York: Pantheon Books.

Scieszka, J. 1989. *The True Story of the Three Little Pigs by A. Wolf*. New York: Penguin Books.

Service, R. W. 1907/1987. *The Cremation of Sam McGee*. New York: Greenwillow.

Shakespeare, W. 1623. *Hamlet*. Available at www.shakespeare-literature.com/Hamlet/index.html.

Silko, L. M. 1967. "The Man to Send Rain Clouds." *New Mexico Quarterly*. Available at https://sites.google.com/site/unitoneoriginsandencounters/the-man-to-send-rain-clouds/text.

Soto, G. 1985. "Oranges." In *Black Hair*. Pittsburg: University of Pittsburg Press.

———. 1985. "The Pie." In *Black Hair*. Pittsburg: University of Pittsburg Press.

———. 2005. *Neighborhood Odes*. Boston: Sandpiper/Houghton Mifflin.

Steinbeck, J. 1977. *Of Mice and Men*. New York: Bantam Books.

Thoreau, H. D. 1849. Resistance to Civil Government: Civil Disobedience. *Aesthetic Papers*. Available at www.walden.org.

Tolstoy, L. 2003. *Anna Karenina*. New York: Penguin Books.

Vonnegut, K. 1969/2001. *Slaughterhouse-Five, or The Children's Crusade: A Duty Dance with Death*. Philadelphia: Chelsea House.

Walker, A. 1973/2003. "Everyday Use." In *In Love & Trouble*. New York: Mariner Books.

———. 1982/1992. *The Color Purple*. New York: Harcourt Brace Jovanovich.

Wallace, R. 2007. *One Good Punch*. New York: Knopf.

Williams, J. 1987. *Eyes on the Prize: The American Civil Rights Years, 1954–1965*. New York: Viking.

Williams, W. C. 1923. "The Red Wheelbarrow." In *Spring and All*. New York: Contact Publishing Company. Available at http://writing.upenn.edu/~afilreis/88/wcw-red-wheel.html.

Wilson, A. 1983. *Fences*. Waterford, CT: Eugene O'Neill Theater Center.

Wright, R. 1945. *Black Boy*. New York: Harper Collins.

Wu, W. 1995. "Black Powder." In *American Dragons*, ed. L. Yep, 211–34. New York: Harper Collins.

REFERENCES

Adams, M. J. 2010–11. "Advancing Our Students' Language and Literacy: The Challenge of Complex Test." *American Educator 34* (4), 3–11, 53.

Afflerbach, P. 2007. *Understanding and Using Reading Assessment.* Newark, DE: International Reading Association.

Alliance for Excellent Education. 2010. *Adolescent Literacy Fact Sheet.* Author: Washington, DC. Available at www.all4ed.org/files/AdolescentLiteracyFactSheet .pdf.

Alvermann, D. E. 2000. "Classroom Talk About Texts: Is It Dear, Cheap, or a Bargain at Any Price?" In *Reading for Meaning: Fostering Comprehension in the Middle Grades,* eds. B. M. Taylor, M. F. Graves, and P. van den Broek, 136–51. New York: Teachers College Press.

Alvermann, D. E., J. P. Young, C. Green, and J. M. Wisenbaker. 1999. "Adolescents' Perceptions and Negotiations of Literacy Practices in Afterschool Read and Talk Clubs." *American Educational Research Journal 36,* 221–64.

Alvermann, D. E., S. F. Phelps, and V. R. Gillis. 2010. *Content Area Reading and Literacy: Succeeding in Today's Diverse Classrooms* (6th ed.). Boston, MA: Allyn & Bacon.

American Educator. 2010–11. "Either It All Works Together or It Hardly Works at All: How a Common Core Curriculum Could Make Our Educational System Run Like Clockwork." [Special Issue] *34* (1).

Anderson, L. M. 1989. "Classroom Instruction." In *Knowledge Base for the Beginning Teacher,* ed. M. C. Reynolds, 101–15. New York: Pergammon.

Applebee, A. N. 1993. *Literature in the Secondary School: Studies of Curriculum and Instruction in the United State.* Urbana, IL: NCTE.

Appleman, D. 2007. "Reading with Adolescents." In *Adolescent Literacy: Turning Promise into Practice,* eds. K. Beers, R. E. Probst, and L. Rief, 231. Portsmouth, NH: Heinemann.

———. 2009. *Critical Encounters in High School English: Teaching Literary Theory to Adolescents* (2nd ed.). New York: Teachers College Press.

———. 2010. *Adolescent Literacy and the Teaching of Reading.* Urbana: National Council of Teachers of English.

Atwell, Nancie. 2007. *The Reading Zone: How to Help Kids Become Skilled, Passionate, Habitual, Critical Readers.* New York: Scholastic Inc.

Beach, R., and J. Myers. 2001. *Inquiry-Based English Instruction: Engaging Students in Life and Literature.* New York: Teachers College Press.

Beach, R., D. Appleman, S. Hynds, and J. Wilhelm. 2006. *Teaching Literature to Adolescents.* Mahwah, NJ: Erlbaum.

Bean, T. W., and H. Harper. 2011. "The Context of English Language Arts Learning: The High School Years." In *Handbook of Research on Teaching the English Language Arts* (3rd ed.); eds. D. Lapp and D. Fisher, 60–68. New York: Routledge.

Bean, T. W., P. C. Valerio, and L. Stevens. 1999. "Content Area Literacy Instruction." In *Best PracticesiIn Literacy Instruction*, eds. L. B. Gambrell, L. M. Morrow, S. Newman, and M. Pressley, 175–92. New York: The Guilford Press.

Beck, I., and M. G. McKeown. 1981. "Developing Questions That Promote Comprehension: The Story Map." *Language Arts* 58, 913–18.

Beers, K. 2003. *When Kids Can't Read: What Teachers Can Do.* Portsmouth, NH: Heinemann.

Blau, S. D. 2003. *The Literature Workshop: Teaching Texts and Their Readers.* Portsmouth, NH: Heinemann.

Bransford, J. D., A. L. Brown, and R. R. Cocking. 2000. *How People Learn: Brain, Mind, Experience, and School* (expanded edition). Washington, DC: National Academy Press.

Brown, A. L., and D. Day. 1983. "Macrorules for Summarizing Text: The Development of Expertise." *Journal of Verbal Learning and Verbal Behavior* 22, 1–14.

Bruner, J. 1977. *The Process of Education.* Cambridge, MA: Harvard University Press.

Chen, Hsiu-Chieh, and M. F. Graves. 1998. "Previewing Challenging Reading Selections for Students for Whom English Is a Second Language." *Journal of Adolescent and Adult Literacy* 41, 370–371.

Clark, K. F., and M. F. Graves. 2005. "Scaffolding Students' Comprehension of Text." *The Reading Teacher* 56, 570–80.

Csikszentmihalyi, M. 1990. *Flow: The Psychology of Optimal Experience.* New York: Harper & Row.

Duke, N. K., and P. D. Pearson. 2002. "Effective Practices for Developing Reading Comprehension." In *What Research Has to Say About Reading Instruction* (3rd ed.); eds. S. J. Samuels and A. E. Farstrup, 203–42. Newark, DE: IRA.

Echevarria, J., M. Vogt, and D. J. Short. 2007. *Making Content Comprehensible for English Learners: The SIOP Model* (3rd ed.). Boston, MA: Pearson Education.

Eckert, L. S. 2006. *How Does It Mean: Engaging Reluctant Readers Through Literary Theory.* Portsmouth, NH: Heinemann.

Eggers, D., and Sedaris, D. 2010. *The Best American Nonrequired Reading* Boston: Houghton Mifflin Harcourt.

Englert, C. S., T. V. Mariage, C. M. Okolo, C. A. Courtad, R. K. Shankland, K. D. Moxley, A. Billman, A., and N. D. Jones. 2007. "Accelerating Expository Literacy in the Middle Grades." In *Effective Instruction for Struggling Readers: K–6*, eds. B. M. Taylor and J. Ysseldyke. New York: Teachers College Press.

Fisher, M. 2007. *Writing in Rhythm: Spoken Word Poetry in Urban Classroom*. New York: Teachers College Press.

Fitzgerald, J., and M. F. Graves. 2004. *Scaffolding Reading Experiences for English-Language Learners*. Norwood, MA: Christopher-Gordon.

Frayer, D. A., W. D. Frederick, and H. J. Klausmeier. 1969. *A Schema for Testing the Level of Concept Mastery* (Working Paper No. 16). Madison: Wisconsin Research and Development Center for Cognitive Learning.

Gallagher, K. 2009. *Readicide*. Portland, ME: Stenhouse Publishers.

Gambrell, L. B., and J. E. Almasi. 1996. *Lively Discussions! Fostering Engaged Reading*. Newark, DE: International Reading Association.

Gee, J. P. 2003. *What Video Games Have to Teach Us About Learning and Literacy*. New York: Palgrave Macmillan.

Goldenberg, C. 2011. "Reading Instruction for English Language Learners." In *Handbook of Reading Research, Volume IV*, eds. M. L. Kamil, P. D. Pearson, E. B. Moje, and P. P. Afflerbach, 684–710. New York: Routledge.

Goldenberg, C., and R. Coleman. 2010. *Promoting Academic Achievement Among English Learners: A Guide to the Research*. Thousand Oaks, CA: Corwin Press.

Graves, M. F. 2006. *The Vocabulary Book*. New York: Teachers College Press, IRA, NCTE.

———. 2009. *Teaching Individual Words: One Size Does Not Fit All*. New York: Teachers College Press and IRA.

Graves, M. F., and B. Graves. 2003. *Scaffolding Reading Experiences: Designs for Student Success*. Norwood, MA: Christopher Gordon.

Graves, M. F., and J. Fitzgerald. 2009. "Implementing Scaffolding Reading Experiences in Diverse Classrooms." In *Language, Literacy, and Learning in Multilingual Classrooms: Research to Practice*, eds. J. Coppola and E. Primas. Newark, DE: International Reading Association.

Graves, M. F., C. Juel, B. B. Graves, and P. Dewitz. 2011. *Teaching Reading in the 21st Century* (5th ed.). Boston: Allyn & Bacon.

Graves, M. F., M. C. Prenn, and C. L. Cooke. 1985. "The Coming Attraction: Previewing Short Stories to Increase Comprehension." *Journal of Reading* 28, 594–98.

Guthrie, J. T., and A. Wigfield. 2000. "Engagement and Motivation in Reading." In *Handbook of Reading Research, Volume 3*, eds. M. Kamil, P. Mosenthal, P. D. Pearson, and R. Barr, 403–22. Mahwah, NJ: Erlbaum.

Hirsch, E. D. 2010–11. "Beyond Comprehension." *American Educator* 34 (4), 30–36.

Hitchens, C. 2010. *The Best American Essays*. Boston: Mariner Books.

Hoyt, L. 1992. "Many Ways of Knowing: Using Drama, Oral Interactions, and the Visual Arts to Enhance Reading Comprehension." *The Reading Teacher 45,* 580–84.

Hull, G., and K. Schultz. 2001. "Literacy and Learning Out of School: A Review of Theory and Research." *Review of Educational Research* Winter.

Jago, C. 2004. *Classics in the Classroom: Designing Accessible Literature Lessons.* Portsmouth, NH: Heinemann.

Johnston, P. 1997. *Knowing Literacy: Constructive Literacy Assessment.* York, ME: Stenhouse.

Kamil, M. L., P. D. Pearson, E. B. Moje, and P. P. Afflerbach. 2011. *Handbook of Reading Research, Volume IV.* New York: Routledge.

Keillor, G. 2003. *Good Poems.* New York: Penguin.

Langer, J. A. 1995. *Envisioning Literature: Literary Understanding and Literature Instruction.* New York: Teachers College Press.

Lapp, D., and D. Fisher. 2011. *Handbook of Research on Teaching the English Language Arts* (3rd ed.). New York: Routledge.

Lewis, C. 2001. *Literary Practices as Social Acts: Power, Status, and Cultural Norms in the Classroom.* Mahwah, NJ: Erlbaum.

Liang, L. A., N. M. Watkins, M. F. Graves, and J. Hosp. 2010. "Post-Reading Questions and Middle School Students' Understanding of Literature." *Reading Psychology 31,* 347–64.

Lynn, S. 2001. *Texts and Contexts.* New York: Longman.

Mahiri, J. (Ed.). 2002. *What They Don't Learn in School. Literacy in the Lives of Urban Youth.* New York: Peter Lang Publishing. New Literacy Studies Series.

Malloy, J. A., B. A. Marinak, and L. B. Gambrell. 2010. *Essential Readings on Motivation.* Newark, DE: International Reading Association

Martin, B., Jr. 1992. "Afterword." In *Invitation to Read: More Children's Literature in the Classroom,* ed. B. E. Cullinan, 179–82. Newark, DE: International Reading Association.

Morrell, E. 2004. *Linking Literacy and Popular Culture: Finding Connections for Lifelong Learning.* Norwood, MA: Christopher Gordon.

National Center for Education Statistics. 2009. *The Nation's Report Card: Reading 2009.* Washington, DC: Institute of Education Sciences, U.S. Department of Education.

National Council of Teachers of English. 2008. *Adolescent Literacy: An NCTE Policy Brief.* Washington, DC: NCTE.

National Endowment for the Arts. 2004. *Reading at Risk: A Survey of Literary Reading in America.* Washington, DC: Author.

———. 2007. *To Read or Not to Read: A Question of National Consequence.* Washington, DC: Author.

National Institute for Literacy. 2007. *What Content-Teachers Should Know About Adolescent Literacy.* Washington, DC: Author.

National Reading Panel. 2000. *Report of the National Reading Panel: Teaching Children to Read.* Bethesda, MD: National Institute of Child Health and Human Development.

National Research Council. 1999. *Improving Student Learning.* Washington, DC: National Academy Press.

Newkirk, T. 2002. *Misreading Masculinity: Boys, Literacy, and Popular Culture.* Portsmouth, NH: Heinemann.

Ogbu, J. 2003. *Black American Students in an Affluent Suburb: A Study of Academic Disengagement.* Mahwah, NJ: Erlbaum.

Olson, C. B. 2010. *The Reading/Writing Connection: Strategies for Teaching and Learning in the Secondary Classroom* (3rd ed.). Boston: Allyn & Bacon.

Olson, C. B., and R. Land. 2007. "A Cognitive Strategies Approach to Reading and Writing Instruction for English Language Learners in Secondary School." *Research in the Teaching of English 41* (3), 269–303.

Pearson, P. D., and M. C. Gallagher. 1983. "The Instruction of Reading Comprehension." *Contemporary Educational Psychology 8*, 317–44.

Pearson, P. D., L. R. Roehler, J. A. Dole, and G. G. Duffy. 1992. "Developing Expertise in Reading Comprehension." In *What Research Has to Say About Reading Instruction* (2nd ed.), eds. S. J. Samuels and A. E. Farstrup, 145–99. Newark, DE: International Reading Association.

Philippot, R. A., and M. F. Graves. 2009. *Fostering Comprehension in English Classes: Beyond the Basics.* New York: Guilford.

Pirie, B. 2002. *Teenage Boys and High School English.* Portsmouth, NH: Heinemann.

Pitcher, S., et al. 2007. "Assessing Adolescents' Motivation to Read." In *Journal of Adolescent and Adult Literacy.* Newark, DE: International Reading Association.

Pressley, M. 2006. *Reading Instruction That Works: The Case for Balanced Teaching* (3rd ed.), Chapter 8. New York: Guilford Press.

Readence, J. E., D. W. Moore, and R. J. Rickelman. 2000. *Prereading Activities for Content Area Reading and Learning* (3rd ed.). Newark, DE: International Reading Association.

Richardson, J. S. 2000. *Read It Aloud: Using Literature in the Secondary Content Classroom.* Newark, DE: International Reading Association.

Rodriguez, A. 1999. "The Boy Without a Flag." In *The Boy Without a Flag: Tales of the South Bronx.* Minneapolis, MN: Milkweed Editions.

Rosenblatt, L. 1978. *The Reader, the Text, the Poem: The Transactional Theory of the Literary Work.* Carbondale, IL: Southern Illinois Press.

Roser, N., M. Martinez, and K. Wood. 2011. "Students' Literary Responses." In *Handbook of Research on Teaching the English Language Arts* (3rd ed.), eds. D. Lapp and D. Fisher, 264–70. New York: Routledge.

Rumelhart, D. E. 1980. "Schemata: The Building Blocks of Cognition." In *Theoretical Issues in Reading Comprehension*, eds. R. J. Spiro, B. C. Bruce, W. F. Brewer. Hillsdale, NJ: Erlbaum.

Russo, R. 2010. *The Best American Short Stories.* Boston: Mariner Books.

Schoenbach, R., C. Greenleaf, C. Cziko, and L. Hurwitz. 1999. *Reading for Understanding: A Guide to Improving Reading in Middle and High School Classrooms.* San Francisco: Jossey Bass.

Smith, M., and J. Wilhelm. 2002. *Reading Don't Fix No Chevies: Literacy in the Lives of Young Men.* Portsmouth, NH: Heinemann.

Snow, C. E. 2001. *Reading for Understanding: Toward an R&D Program in Reading Comprehension.* Santa Monica, CA: Rand Education. Available at www.rand.org/multi/achievementforall/reading.

Soter, A. O., M. Faust, and T. Rogers. (Eds.). 2008. *Interpretive Play: Using Critical Perspectives to Teach Young Adult Literature.* Norwood, MA: Christopher Gordon.

Stahl, S. A., and W. Nagy. 2006. *Teaching Word Meanings.* Mahwah, NJ: Erlbaum.

Tatum, A. W. 2005. *Teaching Reading to Black Adolescent Males: Closing the Achievement Gap.* Portland, ME: Stenhouse Publishers.

Tierney, R. J., and J. E. Readence. 2005. *Reading Strategies and Practices: A Compendium* (6th ed.). Boston: Allyn and Bacon.

Travers, M. 1984. "The Poetry Teacher: Behaviors and Attitudes." *Research in the Teaching of English 18* (4), 367–84.

Trelease, J. 2001. *The Read-Aloud Handbook* (5th ed.). New York: Penguin.

United Nations General Assembly. 1948. *Universal Declaration of Human Rights.* Author. Available at www.ohchr.org/en/udhr/pages/introduction.aspx.

Vasudevan, L., and K. Wissman. 2011. "Out-of-School Literacy Contexts." In *Handbook of Research on Teaching the English Language Arts* (3rd ed.), eds. D. Lapp and D. Fisher, 97–103. New York: Routledge.

Vygotsky, L. S. 1978. *Mind in Society: The Development of Higher Psychological Processes.* Cambridge, MA: Harvard University Press.

Wiggins, G. P. 1999. *Assessing Student Performance.* San Francisco: Jossey-Bass.

Wilhelm, J. D. 2008. *"You Gotta BE the Book": Teaching Engaged and Reflective Reading with Adolescents* (2nd ed.). New York: Teachers College Press.

Wilhelm J. D., T. Baker, and J. Dube. 2002. *Strategic Reading: Guiding Students to Lifelong Literacy, 6–12*. Portsmouth, NH: Boynton/Cook.

Wilson, K. M., and R. C. Calfee. 2011. "Classroom Assessment." In *Teaching Reading in the 21st Century* (5th ed.), eds. M. F. Graves, C. Juel, B. B. Graves, and P. Dewitz, 428–73. Boston: Pearson Education.

Wood, D., J. S. Bruner, and G. Ross, G. 1976. "The Role of Tutoring in Problem Solving." *Journal of Child Psychology and Psychiatry* 17, 89–100.

Wood, K. D., D. Lapp, and J. Flood. 1992. *Guiding Readers Through Text: A Review of Study Guides*. Newark, DE: International Reading Association.